362.1   Krementz, Jill.
KRE   How it feels to
          fight for your life

DATE DUE   PERMA-BOUND

*Biography & Autobiography/
Personal Memoirs*

ALSO BY JILL KREMENTZ

How It Feels
to Fight for Your Life

The inspiring stories of fourteen children
who are living with chronic illness

Jill Krementz

A Fireside Book
Published by Simon & Schuster
New York   London   Toronto   Sydney   Tokyo   Singapore

FIRESIDE
SIMON & SCHUSTER BUILDING
ROCKEFELLER CENTER
1230 AVENUE OF THE AMERICAS
NEW YORK, NEW YORK 10020

FIRST FIRESIDE EDITION 1991
PUBLISHED BY ARRANGEMENT WITH LITTLE BROWN AND
COMPANY, INC.

FIRESIDE AND COLOPHON ARE REGISTERED TRADEMARKS
OF SIMON & SCHUSTER INC.

MANUFACTURED IN THE UNITED STATES OF AMERICA
1   3   5   7   9   10   8   6   4   2   PBK.
LIBRARY OF CONGRESS CATALOGING IN PUBLICATION DATA
KREMENTZ, JILL.
HOW IT FEELS TO FIGHT FOR YOUR LIFE: THE INSPIRING STORIES
OF FOURTEEN CHILDREN WHO ARE LIVING WITH CHRONIC
ILLNESS/JILL KREMENTZ.—1ST FIRESIDE ED.
P. CM.
REPRINT. ORIGINALLY PUBLISHED: BOSTON: JOY STREET BOOKS, ©
1989.
"A FIRESIDE BOOK."
1. CHRONIC DISEASES IN CHILDREN—CASE STUDIES—JUVENILE
LITERATURE.
I. TITLE
[RJ380.K74   1991]
362.1'9892'0092—DC20   91-8253
CIP
ISBN 0-671-72824-5 PBK.

This book is dedicated to
Dr. Kurt Hirschhorn
with much love

Contents

Introduction

This is not a book about children who are dying. It is a book about kids who have faced, or are still facing, serious illnesses and disabilities. They are children who bring to their fight a special attitude that has enabled them to triumph over terrible odds. They have all realized that life is fragile and unpredictable, but they don't feel sorry for themselves and they don't want us to feel sorry for them either.

I chose the title *How It Feels to Fight for Your Life* because that's what these kids are talking about. Some of them have won the fight; some are still fighting. But all of them are fiercely determined to live their lives as others do. They are fighting in hospitals, in schoolrooms, on playgrounds, and in their homes.

I've been working on this book for more than two years. Throughout this time my friends and colleagues have assumed that it has been a sad time for me. Certainly it has saddened me to sit and talk with the children and their parents. On the other hand, it has also been a very rewarding time. I traveled around the country to find and to listen to very *special* kids — kids who are dealing with adversity in ways that would inspire and instruct other sick children and the adults who love and work with them. Ten years ago many of the children in this book would have had little to hope for. Today, thanks to the wonderful advances of modern medicine, they are living fruitful lives with ever-widening horizons.

I didn't set out to catalog all the illnesses and calamities that can befall young people. Instead I have chosen to focus on the emotions and issues relating to quality of life — how these fourteen children and their families cope with disruption and pain. They manage their daily burdens with gallantry and grace. This book is a celebration of their courage and of their lives.

Jill Krementz

Foreword

At least 10 to 15 percent of the children in the United States have some form of chronic health impairment. Of these, at least one million have severe diseases that may require lengthy hospitalization and interfere on a regular basis with the child's usual activities. Furthermore, there are other important sources of severe and catastrophic trauma such as injuries in the home and in sports; from accidents involving automobiles, bicycles, or skateboards; or from assault. Each year more than three million children are admitted to the emergency rooms of our nation's hospitals. Each affected child belongs to a family and each member of the family inevitably shares in the child's struggles. Although many of these conditions can be life-threatening, the large majority of clinically ill or disabled children survive to adulthood.

As one who is acutely aware of how many young people have been affected by these potentially life-destroying conditions, I welcome this book. Jill Krementz presents a sensitive and thoughtful treatment of how some of these remarkable young people are dealing with their disabilities. *How It Feels to Fight for Your Life* will be an inspiration to similarly affected children, to their families, and to the many health professionals involved in their care.

James M. Perrin, M.D.

Director, Ambulatory Care Programs
and General Pediatrics
Massachusetts General Hospital

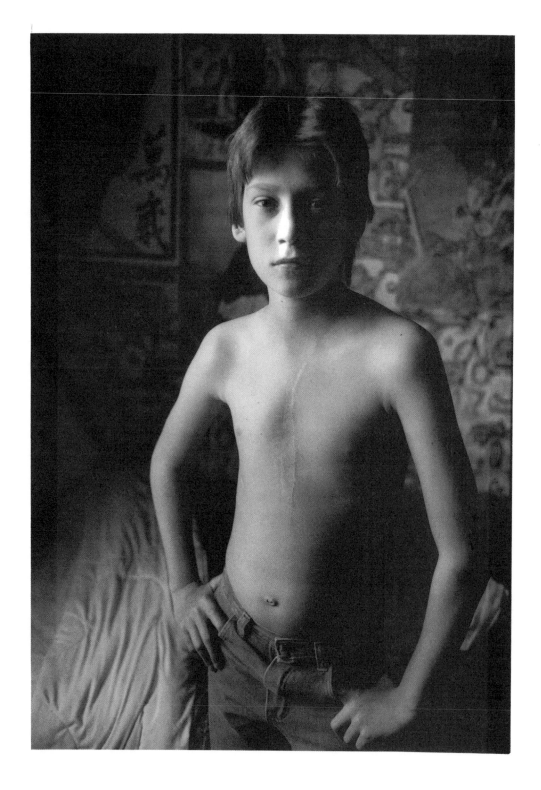

JOSEPH
BUCK

Heart Disease

Before I had my last heart operation I had such a hard time breathing that my face was all blue. I couldn't play with any of my friends. I couldn't run. I couldn't take gym, couldn't ride my bike long distances. My friends would ride me on their bikes. I didn't do much of anything. If I fell the wrong way I'd lose my breath and when this happened I'd get so scared I wouldn't know what to do. When I was in fifth grade I only weighed about thirty-five pounds, even though I ate like a hog. My father called me "T.J.," which means "Tiny Joe." My friends were wonderful — no one ever teased me about being little. I can only remember one time when someone did kid me. He was a sixth grader and he called me "grape face" because my lips were purple, but my big sister MaryAnn straightened him out. She grabbed him by the chest and said, "What did you say?" and he said, "Ah, ah, nothing," and he never bothered me again.

I was two days old when I had my first operation, but I was so young I don't have any memories. My arteries were all messed up and the main artery to my lungs was blocked, so they took a vein from a man's leg and used it to replace some of my own blood vessels. What I do remember is the open-heart surgery I had two years ago. The second operation was needed to fine-tune me and make my heart almost normal.

Even though open-heart surgery sounded scary, I was very excited when I learned they were going to fix my heart. All I could think of was that after I got well I would be able to run and play and ride my bike everywhere. For some reason I wasn't really scared because I didn't know how much it was going to hurt. I just figured that whatever pain there was I would just have to take it, no matter what.

I went into the hospital a few days before the Fourth of July, which meant I had to miss all the fireworks, but I kept thinking about being well and that helped. The night before my operation I stayed up talking with Dr. Golinko, my cardiologist, because he knew how to cheer me up and boost my confidence. He gave me a lucky penny to take into the operating room. It was a 1977 penny because my dream car is a 1977 black Trans Am. And a priest came and blessed me. I'm very religious, so that meant a lot to me.

I don't remember very much about the first few days after the operation but I'll say one thing. Now I know what real pain feels like. Hardly anything hurts anymore compared with what I went through then. I had all these tubes going into my chest to suck the phlegm from my lungs. The worst pain I ever felt was when they had to take the left tube out because it wasn't working, and then shove it back in. Seven people had to hold me down and I was saying every swear word you ever heard of. I was real scared too, thinking, "Oh God — I don't want these foreign objects in my chest!" But after a while I got used to it. The biggest problem was that I had to sleep on my back and I couldn't turn over because of the tubes. I was frightened someone would touch one of the tubes and it would rip out of my chest. I had to be in bed a long time and they exercised my legs to keep them from getting weak. When they were exercising me, I'd always worry about their hitting the tubes.

I was in the hospital practically all summer. After one month they moved me out of the intensive care unit into my own room on the third floor. As soon as I started feeling a little better I had to survive the food they give you. That's another kind of pain! Hospital food is really gross. They put me on a special diet, which for a heart patient means no salt and very little fluids so your heart won't have to work too hard until after it's all healed. It was a diet, all right — I couldn't eat the stuff! You'd think that after all they've done in the way of advancing medical research and designing new equipment, they could be a lot more imaginative about what they give patients to eat, especially the kids. Wanting to eat — and being able to — is an important part of feeling better and getting well. Heart patients are in desperate need of a low-calorie, salt-free Big Mac that tastes delicious!

Speaking of McDonald's, the whole time I was sick my parents stayed in a Ronald McDonald House near the hospital for only ten dollars a night. Our home was a three-hour train ride from the hospital, and I don't know how my parents would have coped otherwise because hotels are so expensive. My mother said it really helped her to be able to share her feelings with other parents who had children in the hospital. Whenever she was feeling down there was always someone to cheer her up. There were times when she helped them, too.

When I get older I'd like to go to hospitals and talk to kids who are getting ready for heart surgery. I'd like to put confidence in them. I'd tell them how glad I am to be alive and about all the great things I can do now that I'm healthy.

Another kind of volunteer work I'd like to do in hospitals is to keep the kids company when they have to leave their rooms and go have X rays or diagnostic tests. One of the hardest things about being in a hospital is all the waiting you have to do for stuff like that. Someone comes and gets you, wheels you down to X ray or whatever, and they just leave you there. It's like being at a bus stop or going to the deli section in a grocery store and being handed a ticket with a number on it. You can wait for hours until they call you. You feel so helpless and so alone and it would be nice if someone kept you company. You could talk or play a game. Anything would be better than the way it is now.

Having open-heart surgery has definitely changed my thinking. One thing I can say for sure is that now I know how to fight for my life and never give up hope. And I know that I can live through an incredible amount of pain. Sometimes I see my friends complain when they get a little bit hurt — when they fall off their bikes or skateboards — and they act as if they're dying or close to it. It makes me wonder if they would have been able to survive what I went through.

When you've been as sick as I have, it makes you grow up faster. And it makes you appreciate what you have. It may sound weird to say this but I don't even mind doing homework anymore because all I can think of is that it's a lot better than being dead. One thing that really bothers me is seeing my parents smoke. It makes me mad because they have good arteries and they're ruining them. I could never abuse my body that way.

All of this has been really hard financially on my mom and dad. After my first operation my parents decided to move to the country and buy a house, thanks to my grandfather, who helped us pay for it.

They wanted me to have fresh air and a place to play outdoors. Mom had to give up her job to take care of me and so Dad works two full-time jobs. During the day he works as a carpenter at Bloomingdale's and at night he works for the Transit Authority. He only sleeps a few hours between jobs and during his lunch break and on weekends. I only see him on Saturdays and Sundays — when he's awake, which isn't all that much. Even though I'm well now, my mother doesn't want to get a job because she wants to spend as much time with me as she can. I guess it's because she almost lost me so now she wants to be there for me when and if I need her. It makes me sad to see how many sacrifices they've had to make but I really appreciated having a full-time mother when things were rough. However, now that I'm much better and I'm in school all day I'd like it if she would go back to work. I think it would be good for her and I know it would be good for Dad and me. My father could go back to working a normal job and I could feel more independent.

I'll probably have to have more operations in the future because I'm still growing and they'll have to replace the arteries as I get bigger and they wear out. I'm sure it will be easier next time because I'll know what to expect. Besides that, they'll probably be able to do it with computers and lasers so it won't hurt as much. I told Dr. Golinko I probably won't need to use my 1977 good luck penny again. That's because by then I hope I have that car. And, if I do, I'll just bring a picture of it with me into the operating room. Or I might bring the letter my sister, MaryAnn, wrote to me on my fourteenth birthday. Even though she's ten years older than me, we're very close. I think of her as my guardian angel. I keep her note to me in the drawer of my bedside table and by now I must have read it a million times.

Dearest Joey,

I never understood your illness until your last operation. I remember when you were seven months old. I was playing with you at Grandma and Grandpa's house. All of a sudden you went into convulsions. I thought to myself, don't die yet — I don't even know you. Even when you were ten years old, I didn't understand what was wrong with you. Why did you cry all the time? I found out years later that you were in constant pain. I wish that I'd been told the truth earlier. Maybe I could have held you more, or held you tighter, to make you feel safe and warm. Since day one I considered myself your other mother. You are everything to me. I couldn't imagine life without you and I won't. You have taught me not to make fun of people who are different, but to look at them as you would look at anybody else. You're absolutely amazing. Not once have you used your illness as an excuse for not doing something. When you were in grade school, instead of telling people why you were always tired or always looked blue, you never told anyone. You didn't even tell the stupid people who made fun of you, including some of the teachers. You never gave them the satisfaction of reacting or crying. I am very proud that you're my brother.

I remember seeing you after your last surgery two years ago. I was devastated to see you hooked up to machines with tubes coming out of your skinny little body. I just asked, Why? Why did this have to happen to you? You didn't deserve this and neither did we. After you had woken up and the tube from your throat was removed, I went to see you and we looked at each other and you held my hand and whispered, "Help me." I thought right then and there I would die. My heart hurt, but I couldn't show you anything. All I was allowed to do was smile, which wasn't easy. Before I was allowed to see you, they tried to prepare us — and all I could think of was PLEASE JUST LET ME SEE HIM. Well, it wasn't the easiest thing to do. From that moment on I finally understood your illness. I still don't accept it, but now I understand it.

Joey, you are a very special kid. Anybody who has met you or who knows you will say the same thing. Even now that I am married and have a child of my own, I still look at you as being mine. And no matter what the future will bring, nobody, and I mean nobody, can or will ever take you from me. I hope we can keep on dancing through life together and that you'll always be healthy. I love you with all my heart.

MaryAnn

BRITTA NICHOLSON

Spina Bifida

I was only twelve hours old when I had my first operation, and I've had fourteen more since then. I was born with spina bifida, which means that part of my spinal cord was on the outside of my back instead of being inside where it belonged. If the doctors hadn't fixed it right away, I probably would have died. The people at the hospital told my mother that even with the operation I would never be able to walk and I might have lots of other problems, like not being able to go to the bathroom like normal people. Mommy and Daddy decided right away that I was a gift from God and they told the doctors to go ahead and fix me up.

The reason I can't walk is because my spine doesn't go all the way down like it's supposed to, so I can't send messages from my head to my feet. If I say, "Feet, move," my feet aren't able to get the word. I can't feel anything from my knees down to my toes.

I spend most of my time in a wheelchair and some time in a stander and a walker. A physical therapist comes to my house twice a week to help me use my stander and walker and exercise my muscles. I have to make sure my clothes are big enough so that the braces can fit underneath. Standing and walking are good for my muscles and keep me from getting heavy. I'd be in trouble if I sat in my wheelchair all day watching TV and eating cookies!

9

Sometimes when I see other people who can walk and run normally I feel bad that I can't really use my legs. My little sister is learning to ride a bike now, and watching her makes me wish I could ride a regular bike. But the people at Gillette Children's Hospital made me a special bike of my own, and now I can have as much fun as Julia.

Another thing that makes things easier for me is my bath chair. Two years ago, my parents got me an electronic chair that helps me lower myself into the bathtub. It makes a huge difference, because without it I can't get in and out of the tub without help.

Between taking baths and swimming, I spend a lot of time in the water! Swimming is one of my favorite things. I sit on the edge of the pool and push myself into the water. I have to flap my arms in order to hold myself up, since I can't kick my legs. Otherwise I'm a good swimmer because my arms are very strong from pushing my wheelchair. My sister has water wings and I'd like to get them, too, so that I can float on top of the water better. I want to swim in the Olympics someday.

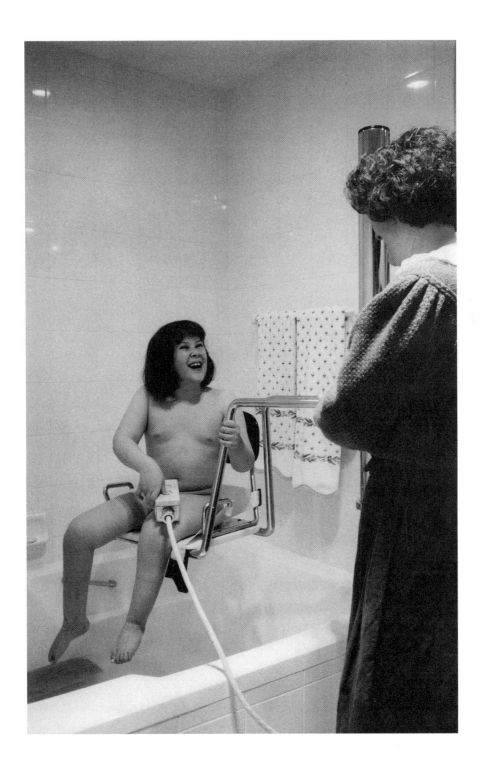

Playing the violin also means a lot to me. When I was three, I said, "Mommy, Mommy, I want to play the violin." And so, at the age of four, I started learning the violin. I've been playing ever since. Julia plays, too, and we practice together sometimes. Since I can't run around with her, it's great that we have an activity that we can share.

I want to keep playing the violin when I grow up, but I'd also like to be an artist. I want to be an artist because I love to draw and paint and because I admire Joni Eareckson a lot. Joni was diving into a pool that was too shallow and hit her head. Her spine was injured and now she can't walk or use her arms. Her book, *Joni,* which tells all about her life, is one of my favorites. Her tape, "I've Got Wheels," is also great — she sings with her students (she's a teacher) about being disabled. Joni has learned to draw by holding a pencil in her mouth. She also got married in her wheelchair!

I'm in a newsletter club that Joni has for disabled children. I write letters to her and she writes back. I've never met her, but I hope I can someday.

One of the worst things about spina bifida is that I have trouble controlling my bladder. This is a problem that lots of spina bifida kids have. Some urine comes out just by me pushing, but other urine stays in. Soon I'm going to learn how to use a catheter. This is a long tube that goes into my bladder and helps it empty completely every four hours. Using a catheter feels a little funny at first, but after a while you get used to it and one day you say, "There's nothing to it" — it feels like normal and it's a piece of cake. I still need a lot of practice before I can use it by myself.

I have to wear Attends in the meantime. These are diapers for grown-ups. My bladder is only one-fourth the size of a normal kid's, but this summer I'm going to have an operation that will make it hold much more urine. Then I'll be able to stay dry all by myself.

Wearing diapers at school is kind of embarrassing. Sometimes they wrinkle and other kids hear it. They're also a little uncomfortable, especially when they're wet.

I go to school every day. In the morning, a special school bus with a ramp picks me up at my house. At my school, they have ramps so that I don't have to worry about getting upstairs. I also have a special desk in my classroom that my wheelchair fits under.

On my first day of school, my mommy brought two books about kids with spina bifida to my classroom so the teacher could read them to the class. We also had the Pacer Puppets visit the second grade and

they put on a show called "Being Different." One of the puppets was in a wheelchair like mine and another puppet asked her, "Why do you go to the nurse's office twice a day?" The wheelchair puppet said, "Well, I have trouble going to the bathroom by myself so I have to get some help. I go to the nurse's office to go to the bathroom."

Now that my friends understand my disability, they have a better idea of what I can and can't do. They know me so well they treat me like any other kid. And this year I joined a Brownie troop.

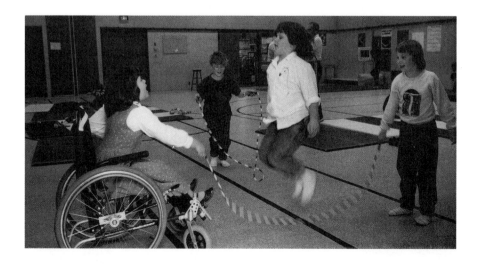

Most of my friends are not disabled, but my friend Andrea has cerebral palsy. One day, I told my mom that I would love to have a disabled friend. Mommy started calling around and asking people if they knew anyone my age who was in a wheelchair. My occupational therapist gave my mom Andrea's number. We have been friends for a year now. When we're together, we play games and watch TV and talk. Sometimes we talk about operations and stuff like that. Andrea has a little trouble walking, but she's very cheerful. She's going to have an operation this summer that may help her walk better.

About a year ago, something very special happened to me. On the night before my birthday, I called my daddy into my room because I couldn't sleep. In the middle of our talk, I asked, "Daddy, what's it like to ask Jesus into your heart?" He said it was very exciting for most people. I decided that I was going to ask Jesus into my heart, so I prayed to God and asked him if he would forgive me for all of my sins. After that I became a Christian. I've been a Christian for one year now. Going to church is my favorite thing to do. I like to sing in the choir, be in musicals, and be in the Adventure Club. When my grandfather comes, I go and sit next to him.

Sometimes I wish I could pray to God and he would cure me, but I don't do it because I know my problem can never be fixed. Being a Christian helps me be a happy and cheerful person and it makes me feel really good about myself. Being able to do so much makes me feel lucky to be alive. I guess I really am a blessing after all!

One night I had the prettiest dream. I was in high school, and we were having a fancy party. I was all dressed up in a white sparkly gown and I was all decked out with flowers — I had a wreath of flowers in my hair and I was carrying a bouquet. I got to dance with lots of boys and we had dinner and everything was beautiful. When I grow up, I want to marry somebody who's like one of the boys in the dream. I won't be able to dance with him, but I will be able to be a very loving wife and mother.

ADAM
ROJO

Leukemia

I have leukemia, which is a kind of cancer that makes things go wrong in my blood. My mom and dad and I found out that I had leukemia when I was five. I've been to the hospital a lot since then. When I first went to the hospital, I always thought a girl had to be a nurse and a boy had to be a doctor. I was wrong. My doctors are both girls.

Every month I have to go to the hospital for a bone marrow and a spinal tap. For each of these procedures, the doctor takes a long needle and puts it in the bottom of my spine. I'm supposed to curl up like a frog and not move to make it easy for them to draw some fluid out of my spine. Sometimes I cry, because it hurts a lot.

The first few times I went to get a bone marrow, the doctors gave me anesthesia. It made me feel awful. So when they were going to give it to me the next time, I said, "Whoa, I don't want it!" I would rather stay awake and have it hurt than be put to sleep. After you have anesthesia, even if it's just local anesthesia, you feel really sick. You can't walk, you can't eat, and you feel woozy. I always throw up when I get anesthesia. If you don't go around in a wheelchair right afterward, you fall down. Without anesthesia, when you're done with the bone marrow you can just go home. That's it. I would definitely tell other kids getting bone marrows not to take anesthesia. It hurts a lot for ten minutes, but then it's over. No sickness, nothing.

I get chemotherapy every week. Chemotherapy is when they put a tube in your body that's hooked up to a plastic IV bag full of medicine. The stuff they give you is very strong, so it has to drip into your body really slowly. When you get hooked up, they put you in bed and you have to stay there while the medicine goes in. Sometimes I have short days, sometimes I have long days that go for seven hours. I don't like long days. While I'm getting chemo, I can only play with boring toys. My mom stays with me, but she can't sit very close to me. All they have is a black-and-white TV — no HBO, no nothing. Normally — like at bedtime — I hate to go to sleep, because when you stay awake, you don't miss a thing. But sometimes I try to sleep during chemo because it's so boring.

Chemo treatments make me feel kind of crummy, but they don't make me throw up as much as some other kids do. I think this is because I try really hard to think about good things while I'm getting them, like going to movies and getting all the toys I want. The treatments make my hair fall out, but it doesn't bother me that much. I don't even wear a hat anymore to cover my head. The only thing I don't like is when I get hair all over my pillow. That stinks. Then I'm lying on hair and it gets in my eyes. And when I pull on it, little hairs fall out, like feathers.

I have to wear a Broviac catheter all the time. This is a long tube that they put under the skin in my chest. The nurses can hook IVs right up to the Broviac so that I don't have to have needles all the time. I hate needles! They hurt! And if you have them all the time for IVs and transfusions, your veins get all collapsed and messed up and the nurses can't find good places to stick you. It's even worse with little kids, because their veins are really small to start with. With the Broviac, you can tell when the medicine is working. When you feel cold, that's when the medicine is going through the tubes into your body. It's kind of uncomfortable.

They can give me all kinds of different medicines at once through the Broviac. The IV bags hang from a special pole that has wheels on it.

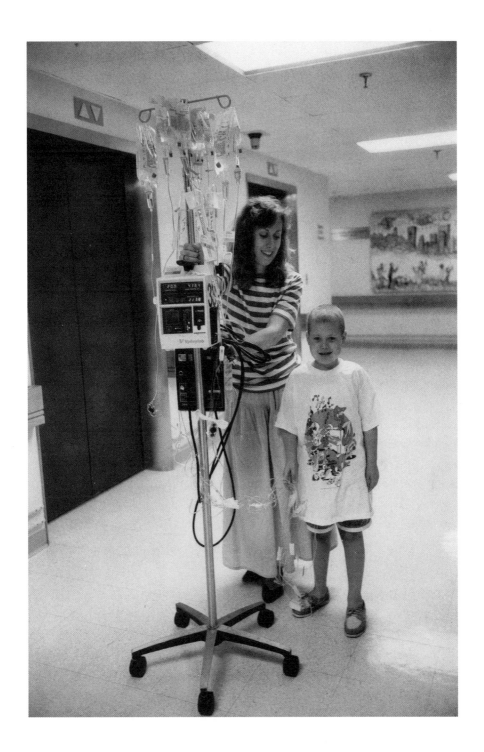

This is so that I can move around and get medicine at the same time. When one of the medicines isn't going through the tubes the way it should, a beeper goes off. Sometimes, when I'm walking around with lots of tubes coming out of me and with the IV pole making beeping noises, I feel like I'm a creature from another planet.

I have to be really careful that I don't get an infection around the Broviac. If it gets infected, they have to pull it out, which is scary. Every day we take care of it. It has to be flushed out with special medicine, and you have to take off the tape and change it. My mom does it all for me.

I can't play too many sports, because with a Broviac you can't fall down and people can't jump on you. It really hurts to get hit there accidentally. I also can't go swimming, because there are too many chemicals in the water. I can't run too fast anymore, either, because the medicine I take makes me tired.

In the summertime, I spent a week at our hospital camp. There's another camp that grown-ups can go to, but this one is just for kids. It's called "Happiness is Camping" and it's in the Pocono Mountains. I had a great time there. The whole idea of the camp is to get you away from your parents for a while and from TV and all that stuff. We had pizza for dinner, and we saw parachuters jumping from planes. My second day there, my mom called. She was pregnant, and she called to tell me she'd had the baby. I wanted a sister, but I got my brother, Max, instead. He's a good kid. He's almost big enough to hold his bottle now.

I have spent loads of time in the hospital in the past year and a half. It's not that bad, actually. In fact, it's kind of fun sometimes. The best part of staying there is that I met my friend Douglas Gonzales. He's a really nice guy. He's a lot older than me — twenty-two. When we shared a room in the hospital, they gave him a VCR and he let me watch movies with him. I try to make him feel better, since he's a lot sicker than I am.

Another fun thing about the hospital is the playroom. We do all kinds of art projects and then they hang them up on the walls so everyone can see them. There are two excellent video games that we can play. We have a whole wall full of autographed pictures of famous people who have come to visit. We also have a newsletter that comes out every three months called *The Playroom Times.* Kids write stories and poems and do artwork. I draw pictures for it sometimes. My dad and I love to paint together. Sometimes Max and my grandmother make paintings, too. The hospital has a special program so that brothers and sisters can visit.

I also like to draw pictures for my friend Roseann. She works at the hospital with kids who are sick like me. She has lots of pictures and stories on her office wall written by kids who were her patients. My favorite thing to read there is a letter written by a boy named Richard Alexander. This is what it says:

When I first came to the hospital I was sixteen and I was very frightened. Just the thought of coming would get me nervous because everybody would be touching me and I would end up having to stay. But once I was admitted it was okay because I got to meet lots of new people, especially ladies. Sometimes it gets really hard to keep going. Once when I was really sick I thought I was going to kick the bucket. But I learned it was just something I had to go through and I did. Now after two years I am amazed that I made it. I am very proud of myself. Right now I feel excellent because I have been through so much and I am still here.

I am living proof that it can be done.

I think that when I'm in fourth or fifth grade, I'll get well, just like Richard did.

We watch a lot of movies in the hospital. Movies are my favorite thing — I like them even better than baseball cards or video games. My parents tape movies for me when I'm not at home. I want to be a movie maker when I grow up. I've watched some movies about sick people, which taught me a lot. The hospital I go to has a videotape with Bill Cosby that is narrated by Meryl Streep. It's called "Your True Colors" and it tells us all about what it's like to have cancer. They give us popcorn, so it's kind of fun. Mainly it tells us not to be afraid to ask questions when we don't understand what's going on. When I need to ask questions I talk to Dr. Wollner. She always listens to me and makes me feel like we're partners. She's great!

My family treats me just the same as when I was well. When I get cranky, my mom teases me and says, "Your warranty is up. We're sending you back to the factory." Or she'll be serious and tell me I'm being too negative. There are lots of times when I'm bad because it's hard to stay in bed for so long and not be in a bad mood. People at the hospital tell my parents that they're lucky I give them such a hard time. They say that if I'm strong enough to fight with my family, I'm strong enough to fight off being sick. When I feel my grouchiest, I just get into bed and pull the covers over my head. That way I don't bother anybody.

I guess my parents give me more attention than my little brother, Maxie, but only when I really need it. They tell me good things, like not to have anesthesia if I don't want it, and they ask me what's on my mind if I look sad. You have to be brave if you have cancer, and my mom and dad helped make me that way. They named me Adam, after Adam and Eve, which makes me feel strong.

The biggest difference between me and other kids my age is I can't go to school. I haven't been able to go this year because I haven't had chicken pox. Chicken pox is especially dangerous to people with leukemia, because it's a weird virus that we can't fight off. My parents got me a tutor so that I can learn the same things they're doing in my second-grade class at school. She comes to my house every day. I like her a lot, but I miss being in school with my friends.

I think it would be dumb if people treated me differently from other kids. I'm the same person I was before I got sick. I can't run or play as much as before, but I can read and sleep and do work and think — most things that everybody else does. When people make fun of me because of my hair or because I can't do sports, I tell them to take a hike.

Sometimes I pray to God and I say that I hope to live happily ever after. I also hope that my brother and my whole family live a long life. I would rather not have leukemia, but that's the way the cookie crumbles.

LAUREN DUTTON

Juvenile Rheumatoid Arthritis

I was a baby when my parents found out that I had juvenile rheumatoid arthritis. Most people call it JRA. It means that I have swelling in my joints. Lots of older people get different forms of arthritis, but having it when you're a child can be really complicated. The doctors say that a lot of kids outgrow JRA, but we're not sure if I will.

I never know when my joints will start to hurt. Sometimes I feel fine, but other times I have pain in my ankles, knees, wrists, hips, and neck. Sometimes my stomach and chest will start to hurt, too. It's not just that I ache; the pain is much sharper than that. When it gets really bad, I have to go to the hospital. This is called a "flare-up," and I get them about once a year. When I have a flare-up, the pain keeps me awake at night. I get a fever and a rash and it hurts so much I can't walk. Then my father has to pick me up and put me into a bath. This helps relax my joints. I take lots of medicine during a flare-up, and I have blood tests where they stick me with needles. It can be a pretty tough time, but I usually don't cry.

If I get pains in my chest I have to go to the hospital for an echocardiogram. That's because my heart and lungs become inflamed, and fluid starts to build up in my chest. This fluid can be dangerous and the doctors take it seriously. The echocardiogram is made by a machine that uses sound waves to look at my heart and make sure that everything is OK. When the pressure in my chest makes it hurt to lie down, I try to sleep sitting up.

Most of the time my disease is under control. My responsibility is to take good care of myself. I take medications every single day. All of them taste terrible, but I'm so used to them that I don't complain about it. It's just something I do. A lot of them relieve the inflammation in my joints. Some, like prednisone, are steroids. I used to take prednisone because it would help a lot when I really hurt. But prednisone had side effects. It made my face all puffy. It also took the calcium out of my bones, which made my hip bones soft.

When I was three, arthritis drugs like prednisone softened my bones so much that they caused a compressed vertebra. The vertebrae are the little bones that make up your spine. They run down your back and protect your spinal cord. One of these little bones squished down on a nerve and that caused me a lot of pain. I had to wear a body cast and stay in the hospital. Now I take a drug called Indocin instead of the steroids. It doesn't work quite as well and it is hard on my stomach, but it is better to take than more steroids. We work closely with the doctors to find the right combinations of medicines that work for me.

Special exercise is an important part of taking care of my arthritis. Since I have soft bones, I am not allowed to jump rope or play hopscotch. The best exercise I get is swimming because it doesn't pound on my legs too much. Every Tuesday I go to a therapist who helps me swim. I love swimming. It's a lot more fun than any other kind of physical therapy. Playing the piano is also fun and good for my joints. I practice every morning for half an hour. The more I exercise my hands and legs, the less chance there is that they'll get weak and stiff.

I have a walker and a stroller that help me get around when I need them. I wish I didn't have to use them, but sometimes I can't manage

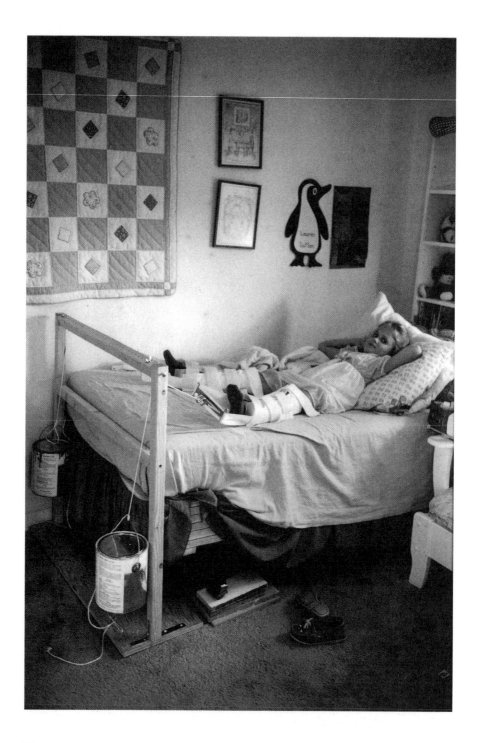

30

without them. I've been going to the same school for a long time, so nobody teases me anymore. They used to think I was a baby because I would sit in my stroller and was smaller than most of them. Now because I can't sit on the floor Indian style, I'm the only kid in class who has to sit on a chair during group times. It doesn't really bother me, but it makes other people curious. I wish that everyone knew more about arthritis so I wouldn't have to teach them.

Every night my parents help me work with weights to spread my legs apart as far as we can. This is because my hip joints are very soft, and we want my leg muscles to be strong and in the right position as I grow. I sleep all night in a contraption that my parents built for me. The doctors told them how. It has paint buckets that weigh a couple of pounds each hanging from either side. I sleep with my legs in braces to keep them straight, and with splints on my wrists. I'm not used to it yet, so it's still hard to get to sleep at night. It's even harder to go to the bathroom because I am so hooked in when I go to bed.

Sometimes I wake up very stiff in the morning and need to soak in a warm bath for a while before getting dressed for school. I like it when we go on vacation, because then I don't have to sleep in the contraption. I know that having to wear those things at night is better than being bothered by them during the day. My doctor told me I was lucky because they used to treat kids with my kind of hip problem by keeping them in traction day and night. Now they realize it's important for kids like me to be with other children in school as much as possible.

At the hospital, there is a special therapy room. That's where they teach me exercises to do to keep my joints moving. It's also where they make the splints for my arms and legs. The therapists mold braces on my wrists and strap them with Velcro. I get new ones every time I grow. I put the old ones on my dolls and play with them.

There are times when I look and feel different from other people. I look different when I'm tired and I get dark circles under my eyes. I also can't always walk the way everybody else does. Most of the time I look pretty normal, but I *feel* different. My moods have a lot to do with how I feel. I work real hard to be in a good mood even if I don't feel well. A good attitude makes everyone happier.

My little sister, Martha, is five years old. She's about the same size as I am, so I'm obviously littler than other kids my age. Martha is my best friend and we play together a lot. When I have trouble with my arthritis she doesn't get as much attention from me or anyone else. This upsets her and she doesn't understand why we don't have more time for her. I try and teach her about my illness. When I have my piano lessons in the afternoon, Mommy sets aside this time for Martha and they play together — just the two of them. It's called "Martha time."

My mom and dad give me a lot of help. Daddy carries me when I need it since Mommy has a bad back. Mommy does a lot of work for the Arthritis Foundation. She travels around the country speaking to people about JRA. Because of this work our whole family got to meet President Reagan. He said her work was important. I'm proud of her for all she does, but it makes me feel sad sometimes, too. It takes up time that she could spend with me.

When I grow up, I want to be a nurse. I want to learn about the things that other people who are sick have to do. It would be fun to be able to help people. If it were up to me, there wouldn't be so many sick children in the world — and the ones who were would get the kind of help I've had.

ANTON BROEKMAN

AGE TEN

Asthma

I've had asthma for as long as I can remember. Even longer. Asthma is a disease that clogs up your lungs and makes it hard to breathe. Attacks can happen anytime. When I have an attack, I wheeze and sometimes I cough so hard I think I'm going to throw up. Every breath becomes an effort — an awful lot of effort. I have to concentrate on taking deep breaths and blowing them out. Usually if I relax enough I can get my breath back.

If I didn't take medicine every day I would always have trouble breathing. I take lots of medication, which makes things easier for me, and now I only get major asthma attacks — or crashes — about once a month. I can't remember a time when I didn't have to take medication every day. I take two pills once a day, one other kind of pill twice a day, and three different inhalers four times a day. Inhalers are like little aerosol cans. I aim them into my mouth and breathe the medicine into my lungs. Each of my inhalers has a different kind of medicine. There's a set of them at school, another set at day care where I go after school, and a set we keep at home. Of course, if we travel we bring them with us.

The inhalers don't taste like anything, but the pills taste awful. When I was little, my mother used to sprinkle my pills — I call them my meds — on jam or butter and I'd take them that way. Now she puts

35

my pills inside gelatin capsules. This makes it easy for me to take them all at once and the capsules are tasteless.

Some of the pills I take are called steroids. Steroids make my body less sensitive to things that irritate the bronchial tubes in my lungs and cause an attack. The biggest problem with taking the meds is they sometimes have side effects. When my doses are being adjusted, I get terrible headaches called migraines. My head throbs and throbs and I feel nauseous. The pills also make me feel hyper and make my hands shake. This can be embarrassing, especially when I'm in school.

When I have a really bad crash, Dr. Greenspan, my pediatrician, gives me a shot. This works a lot more quickly than pills, and when you're having an attack every second counts. I've only had really bad crashes a couple of times in my life. In a way, I'm lucky because my mother is especially helpful when it comes to helping me deal with my asthma. First of all, she's a doctor so she knows a lot about how to take care of me. But even more important, she has asthma, too, and that makes her much more sensitive to small signs that I may need help. For example, she can tell if I start talking or laughing a little differently — it sounds a little as though I'm holding my breath — and she'll say, "Anton, are you getting tight?"

When I was seven, I had such a bad crash that I could have become a statistic. I was waking up every three hours and I couldn't breathe. I couldn't walk more than a few feet without sitting down. Another time I had a fever and chills and started feeling pulses all over my body. All I could do was lie on the couch and pray that I would get better. While I was lying there, I had this fantasy that I was in a wood plane. Little bits of me were being sliced off, until I thought there would be nothing left. I was really scared I was going to die. When my doctor gave me a shot, I felt like all the shavings were stacking up again and I was getting better.

Any sickness makes it harder for me to breathe, especially colds and flus. I stay clear of my friends when they have colds and I get flu

shots one or two times a year to help prevent really bad crashes. I hate getting shots. When someone says to me, "Anton, you're going to have a shot," I feel like running to the best hiding place I can find and staying there. Still, it never hurts as much as I think it will, and I know it helps me, so I try not to make a fuss.

My asthma is pretty bad, about a seven on a scale of one to ten, but I lead a more normal life than some kids with milder forms of asthma. I'm what my mom and Dr. Greenspan call compliant, which means I take my medicine when I'm supposed to.

Every day I do my numbers on my peak-flow meter. We call it a huff-puff. I breath into it and it measures how much air is going into and out of my lungs. My mother writes down the numbers in a notebook. The higher they are, the better it is. We can look at my numbers and tell when I'm going to have an attack. When my numbers get too low, I can usually prevent an attack with Dr. Greenspan's help.

I go to Dr. Greenspan's office often to get what's called a pulmonary function test. I breathe into a big thing that looks like a vacuum-cleaner hose and it tells us how strong my lungs are. Dr. Greenspan cheers me on, telling me to breathe harder.

I used to bring my meds to school with me in a bag every day but now I leave them in the nurse's office. I go there before lunch to take them. One of my best friends is doing a report with me on the respiratory system, so he comes with me. My friends weren't always this interested in, or accepting of, my condition. A few years ago when I would have attacks in school, kids would get scared and run away from me. Some of them made fun of me, calling me "Short Breath" and other names like that. One time a kid grabbed my bag of meds and played "monkey in the middle" with it. He apologized the next day, but it still hurt my feelings. Luckily, my friends believed me when I told them that asthma wasn't catching, especially when they saw how well I could take care of myself.

One of my favorite things to do is play soccer. I play in the town league. I used to play forward, but I stopped playing that position because I had to run too much. It's important that I don't push myself too far when I'm playing, because running hard usually causes an attack. Now I play defense, which is a pretty fun position. You don't have to do a lot of running. You stop the ball and pass it to someone else. My team knows that I have blocked a lot of goals, so I never have a problem getting chosen. I've gotten into the habit of jogging instead of running, but it hasn't stopped me from being a good defender. When you have asthma, it's important to take medicine before exercising.

My mother knows how important it is for me to lead a normal life. This means that I can go over to a friend's house for a sleepover without having to ask if they have pets or rugs in their house — as long as I take certain precautions. For example, two of my friends have dogs. It doesn't bother me too much to play with them as long as I don't kiss them and I remember to wash my hands and change my clothes when I've finished playing with them. If I go on a sleepover I have to bring my own pillow. This makes me feel kind of awkward because I don't want my hosts to think that their pillows aren't good enough. But my pillow has a cover on it that keeps dust from getting into my lungs and irritating them. I'd rather be a little embarrassed than risk having a crash.

As for our home life, we've had to make a few adjustments. We don't have rugs or curtains in our house because they get dusty, and dust irritates my lungs. We also can't use a vacuum cleaner because even though the vacuum cleaner gets rid of a lot of the dust on the floor, when the supposedly clean air comes out, it contains a lot of dust particles that blow all over the place. We use a wet mop instead. The worst thing about not having rugs is that I can't roughhouse with my friends if they come over. It's hard to have a pretend fight if there's nothing soft to fall down on. What I miss the most is not being able to have any animals in the house. If I didn't have asthma I'd have lots of pets — at least two dogs and two cats. I like animals so much. We have an outdoor cat now but that's like having half a pet.

Last year in school we kept journals. I wrote about my asthma. I wrote: "I wish I had no asthma because kids wouldn't run away. I wish I had wings because I could fly." Sometimes I feel really jealous of kids who don't have asthma and I wonder whether I've done bad things to deserve having it. I even get jealous of my mother because her asthma level is so much lower than mine and she can manage it so easily. Sometimes I don't think I can live through mine. When I think about dying, it's because I imagine what it would be like if I had a very, very bad crash, worse than any I've had before.

Still, my real fight isn't to survive, since I usually don't feel that my life is in danger. I am fighting to live a normal life. With the help of my meds and my doctors, I think I'm doing pretty well. But when I blow out a candle, break a wishbone, or see a shooting star, I always wish that I didn't have asthma.

MICHAEL
KLEINEGGER

AGE SIXTEEN

Aplastic Anemia

I was five years old when I was diagnosed with aplastic anemia. That means the bone marrow is not producing as many blood cells as it should. I was on medication for this and seemed to be responding very well, so I carried on a normal life until a year ago, when I was fifteen. Then I was diagnosed as having cancer of the blood. A month later I was admitted to the hospital for chemotherapy and since then I've been hospitalized most of the time. In addition to the chemo, I had to have a major operation on my liver. So they've thrown a lot at me and it's been really, really hard to stop everything and become a bed-ridden person. I'd say it's more of a physical burden than an emotional one because I was an athlete before all this happened. I played football and lacrosse and I did weight-lifting during the winter. I was an active person, so for me just all of a sudden to stop everything and have to lie in bed — that's been the hardest part.

As for the pain itself — and I have a lot — I can deal with it. Even during the chemo treatments, when you get pumped full of chemicals and drugs. I've lost about fifty pounds because my digestive tract is all messed up and my hair has fallen out, but as I said, I can deal with that. I do it by thinking about the end result — getting better. When I used to play football — I was an outside linebacker — I would go into each game thinking about one thing: WINNING! I remember one game when I actually broke my hand but I kept on playing because I hadn't really noticed — I was having such a good time and our team wanted to win so much.

Well, in a way that's how it is for me now. I compare having cancer to playing a football game. Cancer treatment is pain for gain, as the saying goes. It's very painful. It hurts a lot. It does a lot to you. But I've never allowed myself to cry, because there's simply no time. What I mean is, I'm only in the beginning stages of chemo, so if I cry now I'll be crying for the next four months. Why start? I have a lot further to go. There's a lot more pain to come. But I'm ready for it. If I can come back from an operation, two chemos that knocked me for a loop, a lot of time in hospitals, needles, and all that stuff, I can come back from anything. You never cry when you're playing on the football team. You're out there growling and banging heads and nothing can hurt you because you're trying your hardest to win. That's why you're out there. And that's why I'm in the hospital. I want to come out on top and I intend to.

When you're really sick, no matter what your sickness is, you have to accept what's happened and face up to it, no matter what. You have to fight, fight, fight! You're not going to help yourself if you run away.

My schoolwork has definitely suffered. I used to be an average student — upper C to lower B. But now that I'm sick, I'm not doing as well. It's because my concentration is screwed up. I never know what's coming, when I'm going to be sick, when I'm going to be in the hospital, or when I'm going to be home. I don't know when something's coming up at school like the SATs, which are required for college admissions. I like to study and do a little homework when I feel up to it because I *want* to be a part of what's going on at school. I try to do some writing to keep up my vocabulary and, more important, to keep my mind working. Just because I'm sick I don't want to destroy my mind. That's important to me. Lately, since I've been feeling up to it, I've been trying to read, which is good because it takes my mind off myself. You know, you start getting interested in a book and before you know it, you're not really thinking about the tubes that are running inside you, and all the chemicals.

But sometimes it's hard to study, or to do much of anything because they pump you so full of drugs it just knocks you out. You don't remember days on end. I always lose my appetite for at least a week after a chemo treatment. I don't feel like eating and I throw up a lot. And sometimes I have so many mouth sores that I can't eat even if I feel up to it. So maybe it's good not to remember and not to even know what day of the week it is. I tend to just conk out and sleep through the pain, the agony. And oftentimes I get mad and swear a lot. Other times, I think about all the good times I've had with my family and friends and that makes me feel better. You just have to deal with pain in a lot of different ways.

Another way I help myself is by talking to the nurses who are always coming into my room to check the IVs and see how I'm doing. I've gotten much closer to them than to the doctors, probably because they're young and they remember what it's like to be a kid. They tell me I'm a very good patient and that pleases me. If anything's on my mind, it's the nurses I confide in — much more than the social workers or my parents.

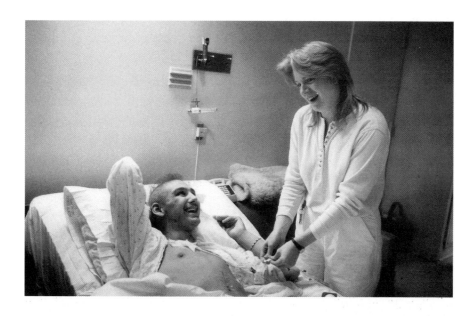

Every patient is assigned to a primary nurse and I've had a great one. Her name is Mary Collins-Pest and besides taking care of me she does lots of little things like bringing me pizzas, sodas, and Gummy Bears. It makes my stays a lot easier. Also, there is one social worker I talk to. I like her because she doesn't pry. She drops by and we chat about silly things and if there is something on my mind I can get it off my chest. But if I don't feel like talking at all, that's fine with her.

I'm hoping to go back to school in a while and I'm looking forward to being with my friends again. I've been back once, so far, just for a visit and it wasn't bad. When I left I was a pretty popular person and when I went back I was still the same popular person — just with no hair and less weight. My friends accepted me just as much. I had been really worried about what people were going to think, but it turned out to be a minor problem — one that I don't even have to think about anymore. It's much harder for little kids to lose their hair because their friends don't understand what's going on, but when you're my age it's easier. People accept me for what I am and not for what I look like.

All in all, my school friends have been very supportive. When I'm in the hospital they call me, or I call them, and it's nice. I love talking on the phone because it cheers me up and keeps me in touch with what's going on in the outside world. One person I've talked to a great deal is the principal of my school. He had cancer himself and pulled through without any permanent problems. It's important to have someone who can tell you what's coming — what's *really* going to happen. The doctors usually minimize the amount of pain you're going to feel, or they avoid the subject altogether — so in a way it's much worse because you're not ready for it. When you expect the worst, what happens is that afterward you usually say, "Hey, that wasn't as bad as I thought it was going to be!" My principal told me that I was going to go through a week of total hell after my first chemo. He said I would throw up so much I would want to die but that I'd just have to deal with it and that it would be over in a week.

He was right. He was told that he only had a thirty percent chance of living, but he pulled through because he fought. He refused to give up, no matter how bad it got. If you keep your spirits up and keep up your fighting attitude, that's half the battle. I'm positive I'll make it.

I did break up with my girlfriend, though, because I felt it would only put another burden on me. I didn't want any additional stress in my life while I was in the hospital, and I knew I wouldn't be able to see her or do things with her while I was there. Besides that, I would always be worrying about her going off with someone else and I don't want to have to think about that kind of thing. So I told her that I had cancer and that we should stop seeing each other. We still communicate all the time but she's able to go out with lots of other people without feeling guilty. That's the way it should be.

I've gotten very close to my family this past year. I'm lucky to have two parents who are very much together because they have each other to talk to and they can cheer each other up when things get tough. It's got to be much more difficult for divorced parents to cope with a sick child. For example, my mom doesn't work so it's easier for her to spend a lot more time with me than a working mother would be able to spend. When parents split up they often both have to work full-time and that would present additional problems. But, as I said, the best part about them being together is that they can comfort each other. And me!

When I'm feeling up to it, the three of us have a great time. My father's a terrific cook and we have incredible dinners right in my hospital room. One night he brought some homemade bouillabaisse and another time he brought in lobsters and we cooked them right here. Even when I don't feel much like eating it's hard to resist his special feasts. It keeps my weight up and the three of us have a good time together. I'm looking forward to the future when all of this will be a distant memory.

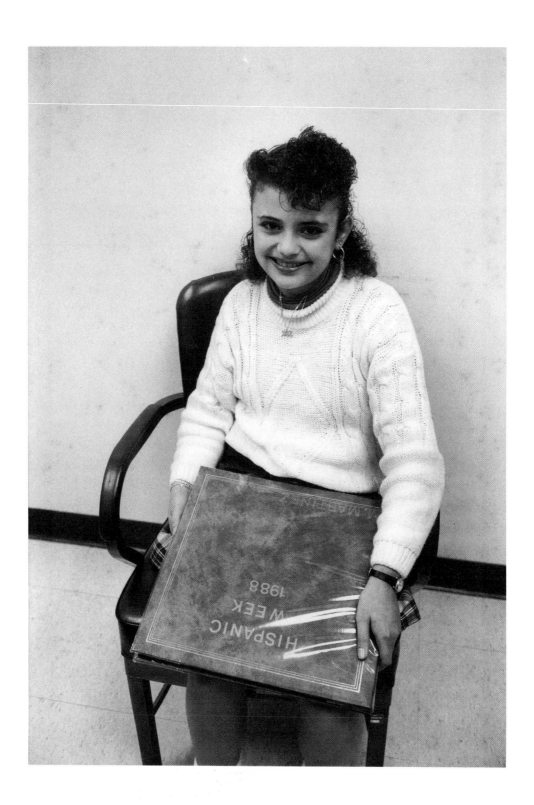

MARYCELY
MARTINEZ AGE FIFTEEN

Lupus Erythematosus

I have lupus, which means that I have an overactive immune system.
Lupus is a rheumatic disease and rheumatic diseases progress through
different stages. It's basically an inflammation of the body's organs.
When the disease is active it makes my joints ache and I get lots of
stomachaches and headaches. I get bad rashes. I feel tired. My hair
falls out when I wash it and when I'm sleeping at night. I have to
take special medicine that has bad side effects like making me gain
weight and have high blood pressure. One of the medicines I take is
prednisone, a steroid, which has stunted my growth. If I didn't have
lupus my immune system would only get rid of bad guys like infec-
tions, but with lupus my overactive immune system can also destroy
some good guys, like my kidneys.

The first sign of a problem was that I had cold hands and feet because
my blood vessels were inflamed. It's called Raynaud's phenomenon.
When I was diagnosed with lupus I was in and out of the hospital for
about a year — mostly in. I was only eight. When I was nine I was
in remission for about six months and that's when I had trouble with
my toes. I got gangrene and they had to amputate the tips of three of
them. I had to have physical therapy for six months in order to walk
correctly again.

The nurse at school has a letter from the rheumatology department in

NORTH KNOX SCHOOL CORP. 49
Junior High

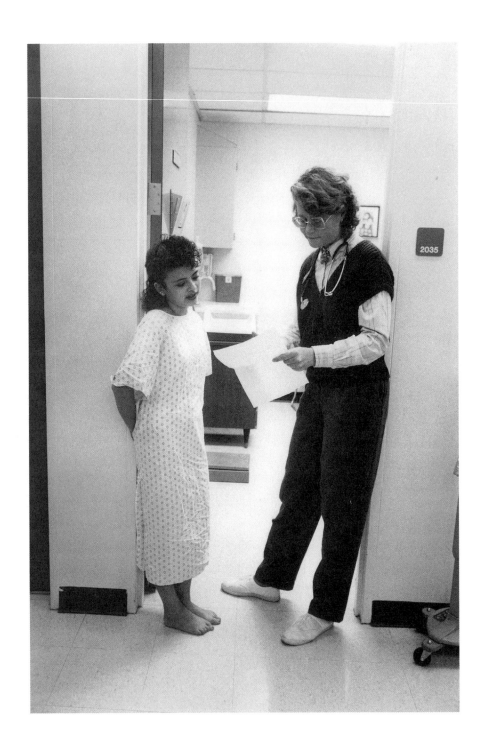

the hospital. She also has my doctor's phone number and calls him if there's an emergency. I look like such a normal person that when I get sick inside, my friends think I'm faking it to get out of class. That's because I'm always going to the nurse's office and staying there for a few hours or I'm going home in the middle of the day. One of the reasons lupus is so difficult to deal with is because it's what they call an invisible disease. On the outside I look like a healthy teenager, but I do have a serious illness that is making me feel awful a lot of the time.

I needed some help with this problem and I got it. This past year I got together with Patty Rettig, who is a rheumatology nurse specialist at Philadelphia Children's Seashore House. That's where I go for checkups or when I'm hospitalized. She made me realize that if I explained lupus to my friends I would get more support from them at school. She was right and things are much better now. Patty invited me to join a teen club, which is an adolescent support group for kids with lupus and arthritis. We meet every other month and have discussion groups about dealing with our diseases. The neat thing about sharing experiences is that you find out you're not alone — that other kids have the same problems with school, with family, and with their relationships. As a result of going to this group I had the courage to tell my boyfriend, Tyrone, that I had lupus and how it affected me. He's been very understanding and helps me with my problems.

Still, school is difficult for me. Because my knees are weak, I can't carry a lot of books at one time. I have to have extra time between my classes so I can go back to my locker and get different books. I wanted to be a cheerleader this year but I didn't bother to try out because my knees were in such bad shape. I have dead bone in them from the prednisone. I'm still growing so it's possible that if the dead part doesn't get bigger and the new bone is healthy, my knees will get better. I'm on a very low dosage of steroids now, so as long as I don't abuse my knees the chances are good. I'd love to be more flexible

— to be able to do splits and to jump up in the air. I'm supposed to exercise for my joints and muscles. The physical therapist showed me how to do leg lifts and side lifts. Patty is working with me on this and trying to help me make exercising as much a part of my daily routine as brushing my teeth. I'm getting better at it. What I am hoping and praying for is that someday I will be able to be involved in sports or cheerleading so that I can be noticed for being good at something and not for just being the shortest girl in the ninth grade.

Dr. Eichenfield has been my doctor since I was diagnosed. I call him

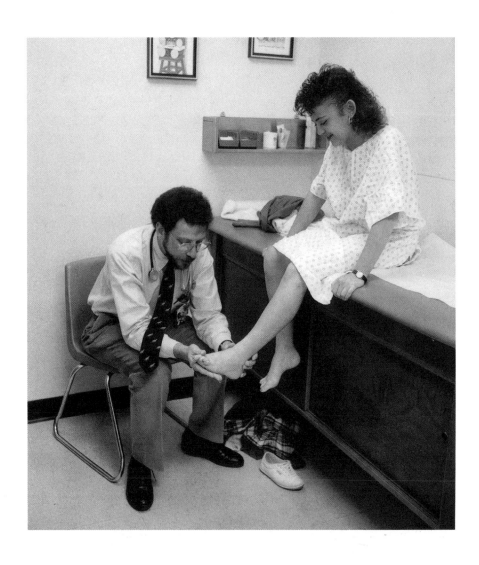

Andy. I have two others. They're all great. Every two to three months I have a checkup at the clinic. With lupus you have to worry about the different things that can happen to you — problems like nephritis, which is inflammation of the kidney, strokes, lung disease, bowel inflammation, brain disease, or kidney failure, which is the most common problem and usually the most dangerous. You name it, it could happen. And sometimes more than one of these things happen at once. And they have. I've been hospitalized quite a few times.

When I'm in the hospital, I concentrate on getting better and getting out. The hospital is so far away from where I live that my family can come to visit me only two or three times each week. My mother works as a glazier in a window factory assembling glass. She works five days, sometimes six. My dad is a mechanic who works on buses. He fixes school buses and works from six-thirty in the morning until two P.M. We have a good medical plan but it still hurts when my mom has to take time off from her work. Because she gets paid by the hour, she doesn't get paid when she has to take time off. So whenever I'm admitted to the hospital it's very hard on the family. It's bad enough when I have to go for a checkup because even then she has to lose a day of work because it's so far away. But she's always cheerful and she always says, "My daughter's health comes first."

Most of the time I'm up and about and dealing with the day-to-day problems of coping with a chronic illness. Some days I have a headache and a stomachache. I don't go outdoors very much. That's because in the winter my fingers and toes get blue and I have to worry about frostbite. I have to bundle up because I get colds more easily than other kids. It's worse in the summer. I can't walk outside because the heat makes me feel sick to my stomach. My skin is very sensitive to the sun so I have to wear sunblock whenever I'm in the sun. When I get my period I feel terrible. Nevertheless, in spite of how I'm feeling, I try to pretend I don't have lupus and go on living like a normal teenager. I get mad sometimes. I don't feel that I should be having all these problems.

It's been a long fight, and day in and day out my mother has always been there for me. At two in the morning she'll give me medicine. When I first got sick I couldn't get dressed on my own. I wish I could outgrow my dependence on her in some areas. On the other hand, I talk to my friends and they don't seem to communicate with their mothers as much as I do. I guess it took my disease to show me just how much she cares about me. That's one good thing that's happened to me. Most of my friends fight with their families for stupid little reasons like "Why can't I go to the mall?" My father hasn't been very involved in my disease, but he's been great. He's the one who carries me if I can't walk and I appreciate that.

My younger sister, Ivelisess, who is twelve, has none of this stuff. She gets frustrated because there are so many things I can't do — little things like jumping rope, playing kickball, or running around with her. She wishes I could be a better big sister, and I wish I could, too. To make up for the things I can't do, I try to buy her things, or walk to the store with her — or talk with her.

Unfortunately, I don't have that much free time to spend with her because I also have a job. I work at McDonald's as a cashier and I help clean up. I do this on weekends and during vacations. I want to learn to be responsible, but also I want to be able to buy a car and be independent. I guess my independence is really important to me because my mom's been overprotective in a lot of ways. For example, I'm not even allowed to go out with boys yet. But last summer she let me go away to the Pocono Mountains for three days because I was in the Miss Hispanic Pageant in Delaware. There were eight finalists, myself included, and we had a busy schedule. Luckily, I didn't have any flare-ups. Even though I didn't win, I had the greatest time. I got to go to new places, meet new people, and experience new things. I plan to run again for Miss Hispanic of Delaware next year. I wrote an article for the hospital's teen club newsletter and encouraged other teenagers with lupus to set goals for themselves and to think positively. It helps me and I hope it will help them.

STEWART
UGELOW

AGE TWELVE

Multiple Burns

It happened three years ago. I was in summer school working on a chemistry experiment with a small group of kids. We were making sparklers and they exploded in our faces. If I hadn't heard voices in the hall and turned my face when it happened, I might have been blinded. I remember it was so hot and everybody was running from the classroom. I was wearing glasses and they were covered with powder. I thought I had been blinded, but I couldn't tell what had happened. A film had formed over my mouth that stuck to my lips and moved with them when I talked. It was all so weird. I had the sense of feeling no pain, and yet feeling a lot — at the same time. They had to cut away the shirt I was wearing because my hands, arms, neck, and face were burned.

I heard a helicopter landing and they rushed me to it. It's hard not to be scared when you're being "med-evacked" to a hospital with another child next to you screaming and a paramedic telling you not to move. As soon as the helicopter landed, they rushed me to the emergency room. Dad was in Ohio on a business trip, but my mom got there after about a half hour. Having her with me really helped.

The pain was terrible. I was beyond crying. It's funny, all I wanted to do was sleep. But they wouldn't let me. They kept asking me how to spell my name and I was shouting, "S-T-E-W-A-R-T. Got it?"

57

They did that to make sure that I wasn't going into shock. I kept asking when I could sleep. I was either hot or cold. They put heat lamps on me and I was too hot, and they took them off, and I was freezing. It was horrible.

Next, they moved me to the ICU — the intensive care unit designed especially for burn patients. There was a high risk of infection, so they started the process of skin grafts as soon as possible. It was clear that my hands had been so badly burned that skin grafts would be necessary. The surgery on my hands took place three days after the accident. My hands had to be elevated all the time after the surgery, so I had to learn to sleep on my back. Later I had two additional operations for skin grafting on my forehead, neck, and arms.

The day-to-day pain was terrible. It was so bad I couldn't think about anything else. I didn't realize how serious my situation was, that is, how close I was to being disabled in a major way. I couldn't have dealt with the pain without the support of my parents. It was never mind over matter, or biofeedback, or anything like that. If they hadn't been there behind me, I would have given up at the first turn, the first struggle. My parents forced me to keep going. My mom stayed with me during the days and my dad spent the nights. They didn't let him sleep in the room at first, so for a week and a half my dad slept out in the lobby on the most uncomfortable plastic chair you can imagine — just to be near me.

I was in the hospital for thirty-eight days. In five weeks, I had to go through three operations for the needed skin grafts. In addition, I had to wear splints on my hands and arms to keep my skin from contracting as it healed. I had a ton of bandages, which had to be changed three times a day. Some of them would stick, which was really painful.

Getting mail meant a lot to me while I was in the hospital. I got a letter from the Washington Redskins that really cheered me up. It said: "We know of your strength and fortitude and we hope you'll

keep your spirits up. . . . Ask any pro player and he'll say that the worst thing is to get down. You must fight for yourself, give 110 percent, and things turn out for the best. Give it your best shot and feel good about that. We're all rooting for you." They sent me a football, too.

Meanwhile, I kept imagining the accident happening over and over again. It was so horrible, it was bottled up in me. I was always fearful that something would happen while I was sleeping, that the hospital would blow up or something like that. The social workers in the hospital were nice, but I didn't like the psychiatrists at all. One day

I woke up and there was this man standing over me. He introduced himself and told me that he was a psychiatrist. He wasn't exactly my favorite person because he would pop in at times when I wanted to be left alone, and he refused to leave unless I talked to him. It was intimidating because I felt I had no control over things. Finally I told my mom that I wanted to describe what had happened and I wanted her to take notes of what I said. Telling my mom everything that happened made me feel better than telling the psychiatrist. I also wrote poems about my accident so that I'll have something to look back on in future years:

THE LONG-AWAITED MOMENT

I was almost home
From a long journey
I stopped to observe around me.
In front of me I saw
With great beauty and splendor
An orange-yellow, fiery mass
* rising in the horizon.*
Suddenly it took hold of me,
And would not let me go.

Then it disappeared, leaving only ashes
And a pain-stricken victim behind.
I felt a chill go down my spine
And felt very tired indeed
Then I saw her tall and fierce,
Yet gentle and loving.

Suddenly I was swooped
* through the air*

Beginning a new voyage.
This time I had only one
* road to choose*
A very rough, unfamiliar
* terrain to cover.*
With pain I realized
That there was a new me.
The only thing left from before
Were my blazing eyes.
On this harder course I
* could feel the heavy*
* gaze of the eyes*
Behind the bushes on the way.
To make it to the end
* of this road of disaster,*
I had to hide behind
* a mask, or so it seemed.*

Since burns take a very long time to heal, I had to go through a lot for the rest of the year. After I got out of the hospital, it took weeks for me to get my strength back, even to get dressed by myself. When

I finally got back to school, I wasn't allowed to go out to recess because getting too much sun might affect the coloring of my skin grafts and because people were afraid I'd get hurt.

My parents had to play the role of the bad guy with me a lot during this time, which was very hard on them. They saw a psychiatrist who told them not to smother me with attention or spoil me. If I didn't want to take a bath, which I usually didn't want to do, my dad would just pick me up and put me in the tub anyway. I'd be begging him to stop and I'd cry, but he wouldn't give in. Sometimes my parents would cry, but they both knew that there was only one chance to get my skin to heal with the best results, and they were determined that everything possible would be done.

Having all this happening at home was very hard on my six-year-old brother. My parents tried to give him a lot of attention, but that was hard because of all my medical care and physical therapy. It wasn't until after I began to recover that we were treated pretty equally.

My face and arms had to be covered with a special pressure garment that looked like a tight stocking. It was designed to maximize healing, minimize scarring, and reduce the sunlight reaching my skin because any sunburn would be very painful and would affect the permanent coloration of my skin grafts. The face mask fit tightly like a ski mask. I had to wear it all day except for eating and bathing. It hurt when I took it off and put it back on because my hair would get stuck in the Velcro fastener down the back. Sometimes my forehead would bleed on the edge of my skin graft and the skin and the mask would stick together, making it really hurt to take the mask off.

When I found out that I was supposed to wear that mask for an entire year, I couldn't believe it. It seemed like forever. At first I refused to wear it and my father had to force me to put it on. We had some pretty big fights about this. He got a couple of punches in the stomach. My parents kept telling me that in a few years, I would appreciate having worn the mask. Looking back now, I see they were right —

the time went quicker than I thought it would and I know it made the scars heal better.

Still, it was a hard time for me. A lot of people made flip remarks about the mask. Adults that I'd never met felt that they could jeer at a little twerp. They'd say, "Oh, Halloween's come late this year" or "Are you from the latest monster movie?" Little kids were scared of me. They would run away when I came into a room. It got so bad that I was afraid to go to the bank with my mother. I thought that people would be suspicious of somebody even my size wearing a mask. I wrote a poem about what it was like having to wear the mask:

THE CHANGE

From my eyes,
What I see,
From my point of view,
Is little beyond me.

Some people stare,
Some go their way,
Some just glare,
No matter what I say.

Some walk by,
Or talk behind my back.
Some just look at the sky,
Some think brains I lack.

But there are a few,
They know me,
Just like you,
Who treat me like they want to be.

I wear a mask,
Am I better now?
 people ask,
When I say yes,
They all say "wow."

I think the accident has made me a bit more independent than somebody my age would normally be. Even though my parents backed me up, it's a fight I had to make on my own. Their support helped me but it didn't win the emotional battle for me. I had to do that for myself.

The biggest thing I've had to deal with is my fear of fire. At first, I couldn't even stay at birthday parties when the cake came. Then I realized it wasn't doing me any good to run away, and I forced myself to sit there while they blew out the candles. Recently, I went to dinner at Benihana's. I had to prepare myself for it because the flaming oil used for cooking on the grill made me afraid that if there was a fire, my family and I wouldn't be able to escape. When we were done, I saw that I could control my fears to some extent. I even had to work at watching movies with fires in them. When I was in the hospital, there was a movie on TV that ended with a bombing and a fiery plane crash. It gave me nightmares for a week, but in the end it helped me fight my fears.

In some ways this experience has shattered my innocence. I lost any hope of believing in religion. I ask myself, "If there's a God, why would he do this to a nine-year-old?" If there's a mighty and powerful creator who controls the world, he wouldn't let things like this happen. Sometimes I get angry that this happened to me, and sometimes I get sad. Other times I don't mind it at all.

My life is a fight — against my fears and for my future. It's not easy right now, but the worst will all be over in a year or two. I'm pretty sure that I'll never walk into a singles bar and have somebody say, "Ooh, you're so handsome." But in the course of the next few years, I'll probably have a few more operations to smooth out some of the scars.

For all I know, the scars will be for an eternity. But I feel that if I know somebody really well and they know me, my scars shouldn't be a barrier.

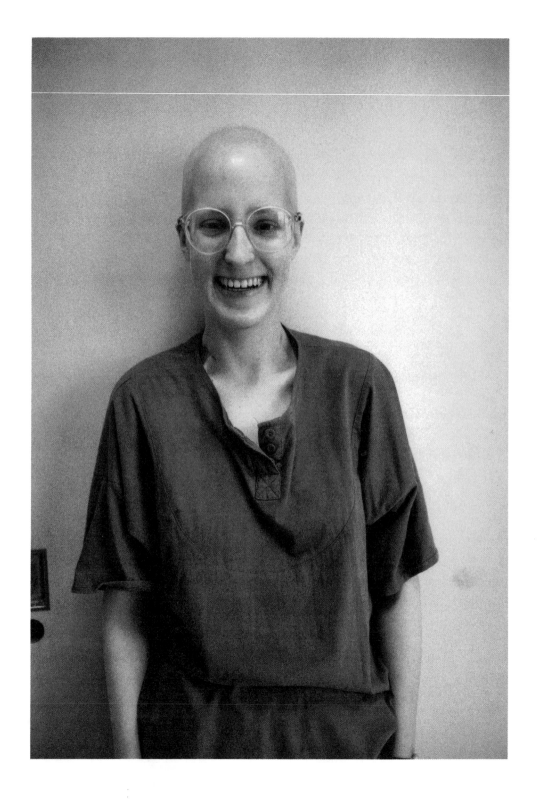

ELIZABETH
BONWICH

AGE SIXTEEN

Osteogenic Sarcoma

It took the doctors close to a year to diagnose my disease. On Christmas Eve in 1986 I was hanging out with my friends at South Street Seaport in New York. We were standing outside eating ice cream and just after we went inside the index finger on my right hand started hurting. I didn't bang it. I didn't do anything to it. It just got really painful.

The following day I went to the doctor for X rays and it turned out there was a hole in the bone that had caused it to fracture. No one could figure out what it was. They thought maybe it was an infection but they weren't sure, so they biopsied my finger. That was inconclusive, so a bone scan was the next step. First the doctors injected my body with a radioactive fluid that's absorbed by the bones, and they put me in this big machine that moves from your head all the way down to your feet — front and back. When the radiologists looked at the bone scan, they found a strange spot on my kneecap.

The doctors performed a biopsy on my kneecap by removing a little piece of it. When they examined the tissue they were even more confused. I had the top pathologists in the country looking at my slides, but none of the doctors could agree what it was. Half said it was osteogenic sarcoma, or bone cancer, and the other half said it wasn't. Some of them advised me to have my kneecap taken out. They said that if I didn't have it removed I would die. Finally, my parents and I decided there wasn't enough evidence of cancer for me to have the surgery, but I was already starting to get pretty nervous.

When they told me they thought it was cancer, I went to the library and did a lot of research — the same way I would for a term paper. I started with a book from the American Cancer Society and went on from there. Since it wasn't a hundred percent certain that I had cancer, my mother was always asking me, "Why are you doing all this research? You might be perfectly OK." But I figured that if I really did have osteogenic sarcoma, I wanted to learn as much as I could while I still had the time and energy and while I was relatively calm and collected. Even now I go and look up procedures so I can better understand what's happening to me. The doctors don't always tell you all that you want to know. I've learned to ask a lot of questions when I talk with them. And to try to find information from other sources, too.

Doing the research was reassuring because the only cancer book we had at home was really outdated. It said that osteogenic sarcoma was fatal about half the time, and that the only treatment for it was amputation of the cancerous limb. I was totally freaking out about that, but once I found more up-to-date material I learned that chemotherapy works well in many cases and that if I did have to have my knee removed, the joint could be replaced surgically.

About three months after I had my kneecap biopsied, the doctors took more X rays. The main pathologist, who originally said it was malignant, came in and looked at my knee and said, "Well, it's definitely not malignant because it hasn't grown." He said that if it was cancerous there would have been a tumor on my knee the size of a baseball. There was nothing there. I was fine as far as everyone was concerned. My surgeon started joking and calling it "Bonwich Disease."

That September I was bowling and I broke the same finger a second time. I was surprised because my finger hadn't bothered me that much. But then, without any warning, it suddenly snapped. It was terrible. After this, they rebiopsied both my finger and my kneecap and the results were sent to all the same pathologists who had seen the original stuff. It turns out that a tumor had grown on the inside of my finger and had weakened the bone. By Thanksgiving everyone agreed. I had cancer.

Osteogenic sarcoma is a disease that particularly hits teenagers and people in their early twenties. It generally gets you in the femur and tibia, the bones in your leg. My doctors told me that it was very rare to have it in the kneecap. It was because I got it in such bizarre places that they'd had so much trouble diagnosing it. They told me that they would have to remove my finger and my knee and that I'd have to have chemotherapy for about a year.

When I learned that I was going to lose both my finger and my knee, I was sure that the surgery was going to be the worst part of having cancer. I thought, "I like my fingers. I'm attached to them. I don't want anyone to take one away from me!" But before they could even perform the surgery I had to have chemotherapy to reduce the size of the tumors. As soon as I went to the hospital and saw all the bald people who looked so sick all I could think was, "Is this going to happen to me?" I started dreading the chemo as much as, if not more than, the amputation.

The first step in chemo is deciding whether you want to have a Broviac, which is a plastic tube, put into your chest. It's inserted into a vein that leads right into your heart. If you don't have one the drugs have to be injected through your veins and you have to have needles stuck into you constantly. After a while your veins collapse and get black and ugly-looking. On the other hand, a Broviac has to be inserted surgically and it requires very special care. Otherwise, you get an infection. You can't go swimming with a Broviac because the water is full of bacteria, which could cause infection. Contact sports are out. I was having a hard time deciding what to do, so my doctor arranged

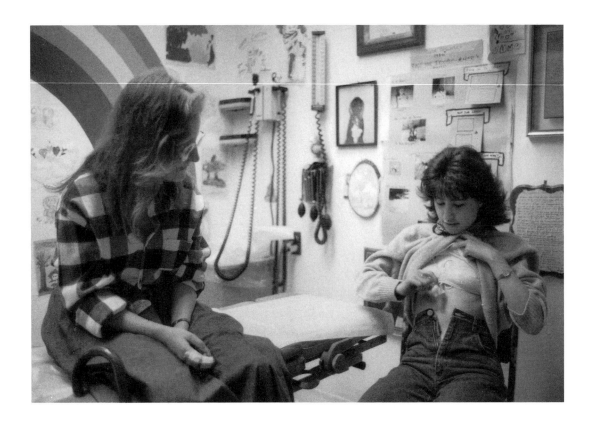

for me to meet another cancer patient named Özlem. It was great having someone my age to talk to because when you first start going to the hospital you're scared and you don't know what's going on. If you get sick and are suddenly thrown into a situation where strange people are poking at you, asking personal questions, sticking needles into your arms, and telling you why they want to put a plastic tube into your chest, it's really overwhelming.

Özlem had just completed her chemotherapy and she gave me a lot of good advice. She showed me her Broviac, since I didn't know what one looked like, and she told me I should *definitely* have one. She had resisted at the beginning, and, as a result, most of the veins in her arms were a complete mess. One look at them and I was convinced. So I got a Broviac but I didn't have it for long, unfortunately, because

I got a bad infection and the doctors had to remove it. They replaced it with another device called an Infusaport. It's a disk inserted under the skin that is attached to a tube leading into my heart. When I need chemo, the IV nurses stick a needle through my skin into this disk. It hurts more than having a Broviac but I like it better because I don't have to deal with all the upkeep that goes with a Broviac. Also, I can go swimming and take showers. The pain is minimal — just a pinprick — so it's well worth the trade-off.

Özlem also helped me deal with one of the worst parts of chemotherapy — losing my hair. The drugs they give you are toxic, which is why your hair falls out. When Özlem pulled off her wig, I was flabbergasted! I didn't realize she was wearing one. That's how good it

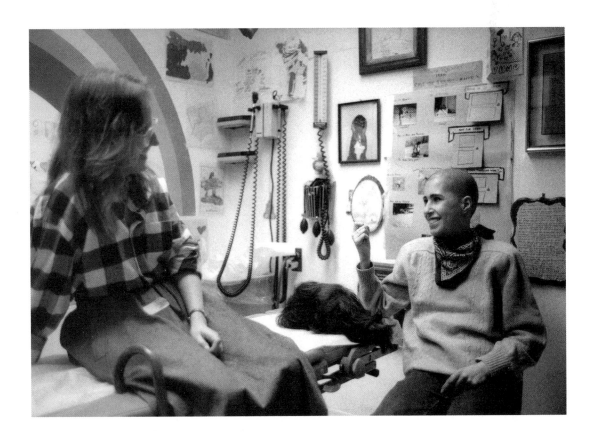

looked. She told me to wait until I lost most of my hair before I even tried one on. That way the wig fits your head perfectly and besides looking better, it's more comfortable. I had been planning to buy a wig immediately, before losing even one hair, so that I would be ready. I'd have to say that meeting and talking with Özlem was one of the best things that happened to me during those first few days after I had started my general treatment.

For me, the weirdest thing about chemotherapy is the thought that you're being infused with potentially lethal amounts of drugs. It's difficult to sit in the hospital and see a bottle suspended from the ceiling and realize that there are toxic chemicals coming into your body. For one type of chemo, they give you an antidote twenty-four hours after they give you the original drug, and then they test your blood to see how much of the drug is left in your system. After that you have to sit in the hospital for six to eight hours a day for two to three days while they pump you full of IV fluids. It's called hydration.

They give you a schedule of treatments called the protocol. It tells you what drugs they're giving you for each week of your treatment. Mine was scheduled for thirty-six weeks with two weeks off for surgery. Some chemos are worse than others and there are two that everyone dreads — cisplatin and Adriamycin. They both make you very nauseated. In fact, these two treatments made me throw up nonstop for four or five hours. I had five chemotherapy treatments before I had the operation on my knee and finger.

The surgery itself wasn't as awful as I had expected it to be. The two procedures were performed by two different surgeons during the same operation. And the pain wasn't as bad as I expected. What I really wasn't prepared for, emotionally, was how I would feel about the loss of my knee and my finger. It's not as if anyone could have prepared me because they couldn't have. Like a lot of other things in life, you just can't realize how it's going to feel until after it's happened. For example, when they took out my knee, the surgeons put a metal rod in my leg so I can't bend it anymore. This makes it hard to get around and do things that I used to. If I go to the movies I have to go to an early show so I can have an extra seat to put my leg on. And getting in and out of cars is a total pain. Once I'm in, I need the entire back seat. As for my finger, I still have phantom sensations and those are difficult to deal with. I had to relearn how to do a lot of things I used to take for granted such as cutting my meat and writing.

On top of all this, I lost my hair — all of it. It was really grim. I'd find it on my pillow when I woke up, it would shed all over my clothes, go down the drain when I took a shower, and went everywhere when I brushed my hair. Somebody told me to cut my hair short before I started, but I wanted to keep all my hair for as long as I could. I realize now that I should have cut it short before beginning the chemo.

I never thought it would be as bad as it was. When you have long hair you have so much more of it to lose. After it started falling out, I stopped combing and brushing it. I put on a little paper cap like the ones they wear in surgery, and let my hair get all matted. Eventually, one of the nurses came in and said, "You can't keep doing this!" and she cut off most of what was left. After that, I looked really evil. I was kind of gaunt, and my cheeks were all sucked in. I had circles under my eyes and very thin, wispy hair.

After surgery, my hair grew in a lot. It was great. I could go out in the street and no one would think it looked strange. But when I started chemo again two months later, my hair started falling out again. This time I said, "Either it's here or it's gone." I didn't want it falling all over the place so I started pulling it out gently.

I'm totally bald now. If I'm going out of my house I wear a scarf, or, if I'm cold, I wear a hat. Most of the time I don't bother with anything because it's more comfortable. I did go to an excellent seminar called "Look Good . . . Feel Better" where they had various experts

talk to us about makeup and wigs. I tried on one of the synthetic wigs and it looked so good they gave it to me as a present. My hair won't be growing back until I've finished with my chemotherapy.

Ideally, the chemo protocol takes about nine months, but most people take around a year to complete it. For me, the cycle of treatments has taken a super-long time because in the beginning my body couldn't tolerate some of the drugs and I needed time to recover before getting additional doses. Before I had my first chemo, they told me, "This particular medicine probably won't make you that sick." I went home from the hospital and since I didn't feel that bad, I ate a big ravioli dinner. A couple of hours later, I felt so awful, I threw up all over the place. I've never had a chemo that wasn't accompanied by nausea, though some are definitely worse than others.

I lost about twenty pounds in the first three weeks, not only because of the vomiting, but because the drugs give you terrible sores in your mouth and throat. When you have them, you can't eat, you can't swallow, you can't brush your teeth, you can't talk — nothing! It was really bad. They warned me about the nausea, but no one ever mentioned the mouthsores, which were horrendous.

At one point, I thought about smoking marijuana to take away the nausea. I asked my oncologist — the doctor in charge of my chemotherapy — whether this was a good idea. She suggested I not do it. She said it messes up the cells in your body, not to mention your mind, and that I should stay away from it. I've had so many drugs that I didn't want to start taking any more. I'll never understand why drug addicts think morphine's so wonderful. It makes me feel terrible.

Finding a doctor you feel is right for you is really important. That relationship is the basis for your whole treatment. Like any relationship, what's right for one person isn't always good for another. If you have cancer, you want to feel close to your oncologist. I ended up switching doctors in the middle of my treatment, right after my surgery and before my long follow-up course of chemo. I didn't feel that

I had a particularly good relationship with my first doctor and I thought this would be a good time to change since I had the major part of my chemotherapy left to go. I wanted to work with Dr. Meyers because I had seen him in action. I had also seen a lot of Karen, his nurse-practitioner, and I liked her a lot, too. My parents did most of the talking with my first doctor about making a change. It was an awkward situation and I wouldn't have known what to say. My first doctor was very understanding. She offered to get in touch with Dr. Meyers and discuss my case and records. I had contacted Dr. Meyers in advance to make sure he could take me. I think I made the right decision even though it was a little embarrassing. I like Dr. Meyers a lot and so far he seems right for me.

Being in the hospital so much has been rough. It seems that all they ever talk about is germs. Chemotherapy destroys the white cells in the blood, which is why cancer patients have very little resistance to illness. I know a lot of people who have gotten pneumonia after having chemo; a couple of other people got tuberculosis. It can get into your blood. One friend of mine ended up in the hospital for three weeks, on heavy antibiotics, because he was infected with bacteria that probably weren't enough to give a healthy person a cold.

Because of my low white cell count, I can't go to school. When I first told my friends I had cancer, they were really shocked. Some of them started behaving differently toward me. Now I rarely see my friends. I mainly talk to them on the telephone. They've helped me a lot. But since I don't spend a lot of time with them, I feel like I'm out of touch. Last June I went back to school for a couple of days to visit. We dissected a fetal pig in biology, my favorite class. Afterward, I heard that a girl had said I had come back to say my good-byes. That was ridiculous, since I'm hoping to be back in school for good in about six months. Sometimes I wonder if other stories like that are going around at school. Most of the time I don't want to know.

I've met a lot of nice people at the hospital. It's a lot better in pediatrics. The adult floors are dead. It's as though a cloud of doom is hanging over the patients' heads. Since I'm an only child, it's nice to be around people my own age. When I had my finger biopsied, I met a girl who had gone to the same school as I and was having some work done on her knees. We got to be close friends, which was fun. It was during New Year's, and there weren't too many people in the hospital. There were only about seven people in the pediatric ward and we all got to know each other. In spite of our muscle spasms and our pain medication, we had a good time. We'd discuss the cutest residents and compare our experiences in the hospital.

When I was in over Thanksgiving, one girl started making a list. She was having serious pain and muscle spasms, and her doctor hadn't told her this would happen. She was furious and she said, "What do I have to be thankful for? Muscle spasms, doctors who don't tell you everything, nurses who don't — or can't — come when you call, bedpans. . . ." She went on and on. It was absolutely hilarious, if you like black humor. And if you're going to spend a lot of time in a hospital, you need to have a weird sense of humor.

Another nice person I've met and gotten to know is Joe Kerest. He's the high school teacher from the Board of Education who helps me

keep up with my schoolwork when I'm in the hospital. I usually study with him while I'm having my hydration or even while I'm having my chemo if it doesn't knock me out. Sometimes I tell him I'm too sleepy but he says, "That's okay, kids sometime sleep in regular school, too." Even though I've been out of school for over a year, I can get full credit for attendance if I work with him. Last year I got promoted to the eleventh grade on the basis of my marks. I passed all my Regents exams with flying colors. In fact, I got a perfect score on my biology Regents. And if all goes well this year I should be able to rejoin my class next fall.

Because of my illness, I am seriously considering becoming a doctor. I love science. It's my favorite subject. I especially love dissections. Once, in school, before I got sick, I was working on a sheep heart with two other people, and they said, "You look like you're enjoying yourself. Ugh! You're touching it!" I've always enjoyed that sort of thing, so I'm thinking of becoming a surgeon. One of the requirements for a medical degree should be to have had a serious illness. It makes a big difference in the way you look at things.

Once I get through my own treatment I'd like to help others who are about to start treatment and are scared and worried — just like Özlem helped me. Talking with Özlem was something I'll never forget. All hospitals should try to set up patient-to-patient discussions. Another way to be in touch with other kids is through our newspaper at the hospital school. It's called *Rolling Sloan,* because the place where I have my treatments is called Memorial Sloan-Kettering. This is the third year they've had the paper. There's an advice column in the paper that used to be called "Dear Melissa." Melissa, the girl who initially wrote it, answered serious questions about hospital stuff. Her answers were really good; they were very sensitive. When she finished her treatment, I took over the column. Now it's called "Dear Elizabeth." It's great! I just answered my first letter. The kid who wrote to me wanted to be alone in his room at the hospital, but people would always come in and want to talk to him. His dilemma was that he couldn't tell people that he didn't feel like talking to them without being rude. I gave him three things to try that I use. First, to keep his doors and curtains closed. That's a big deterrent. If that didn't work, I told him to try a "Do Not Disturb" sign. And if all else fails, there's the "heavy eyelid" method. That's where you start opening and closing your eyes as if you're drifting off, but act as though you're fighting to stay awake and listen. Since everyone there is aware of the way medications can make you feel, they'll usually leave you alone so you can have time to yourself.

It took me a long time to sort out this privacy question, because it's so similar to a problem I have myself. When I go into chemo, I like having someone with me. I need somebody to help me with my bed-pan or my throw-up dish, or to raise my feet, or to get me blankets and pillows. My mother is always great about running errands and comforting me. I love having her around when I'm feeling sick, but when I'm feeling better sometimes I feel she stays at the hospital too much. It ruins my social life, because if I'm in a friend's room or I'm cruising around somewhere, she'll always come and get me. At night, if I turn over or shift the blankets, she'll wake right up and ask me, "What's the trouble? What's wrong?" Sometimes I'd rather have my place to myself. It's hard on both of us.

My father is a different story. I feel that he doesn't get involved enough with my illness. For example, at the end of June I had chemo. I was getting Adriamycin, which is red. I'd been through this a lot of times before, since I'd been on chemotherapy for seven months. My father was sitting in my hospital room and I had the Adriamycin dripping into me. He looked up and said, "What's that red stuff? Is it medicine?" He should know that the red stuff dripping from my IV pole is medicine. Little things like that are not much to ask. On the other hand, he's so busy working and trying to make ends meet financially that I can see how it's difficult for him to be as involved with my sickness as I'd like him to be.

I cry a lot at night when I'm alone. My mother is very supportive, but I feel that if I cried to her, she'd get upset and I would feel even worse. Lots of people at the hospital look at me and say, "Wow, she's got a great attitude. She smiles all the time." I think, "Yeah, you should see me at night!" Sometimes I can only sleep during the day when the lights are on and people are around. When everyone is asleep and it's all quiet, I'm wide awake. I listen to the radio for hours, and I can't go to bed without watching David Letterman. I read a lot, too. If you came into my room at two o'clock in the morning, you'd probably see me sitting there with my guide to colleges.

Part of my problem with sleeping is that sometimes I feel that I'll go to sleep and won't wake up. I always have the fear that something bad is going to happen because a lot has gone wrong in the course of my treatment. For example, when I first started my chemo drugs, my body reacted so badly that I ended up in intensive care. That was in January. Six months later the count of the platelets in my blood was so low that I needed to have multiple transfusions. A normal platelet count is above 300,000. Mine was only 1,000. They usually transfuse you when they're under 20,000. So much has gone wrong for me that I've had to deal with a lot of unexpected trauma.

It's hard not to be scared when I've seen so many of my friends die. That's the worst part of having cancer. Since I've started my treatment, fifteen people I know have died. It's horrible to come into the hospital and say, "How is So-and-so doing?" and have the doctor or nurse look at you and say, "Well, I have bad news." They're pretty honest about that. Or sometimes you don't see someone for a while and you kind of guess what happened. I hate that. For a while, I avoided spending time with people who had more fatal kinds of cancer, but now I'm getting close to a couple of them. I always try to visit my former roommates and friends if they're in the hospital and I'm there as an outpatient. I know how it feels to be lying in bed alone and in pain and then suddenly have someone I care about

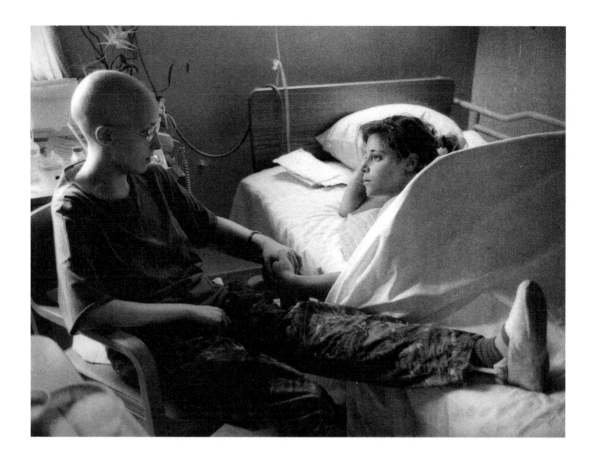

come in to visit. It's good to be able to do that for someone else when I can.

Last summer I went to a camp with all kinds of pediatric cancer patients. Most of them were off treatment, so it was a nice break from being in the hospital. There were only two bald people in a group of sixty, me and another kid. I liked it there, but they had strict rules. They wouldn't let you go anywhere without a counselor. It's humiliating when you're sixteen years old and you can't walk down the road or be in your cabin by yourself without a counselor. But I actually got along with the counselors better than with the kids. A lot of them had been going to camp together forever and ever. They had their own group of people that was hard to break into. Still, the camp was beautiful and it was good for me to be able to be apart from my parents for a while — and them from me. It gave them a chance to catch their breaths and get caught up on all the things they had put on hold. I doubt if I'll go back next year. That's because I'm hoping to go to Australia as an exchange student. I wanted to do that last summer but my plans got messed up by my chemo treatments.

My surgeon, Dr. Lane, is going to wait until I get my strength back and pull myself together after the chemo before he starts joint replacement surgery on me, which will make it possible for me to bend my leg again. He believes that the cancer in my leg should be completely cured when I finish the chemo and that we should wait until then. I really want to have it done before I go to college.

I'm also hoping to work with Paddy Rossbach in the not-too-distant future. She has a program at The Hospital for Special Surgery called ASPIRE — Adolescent Sarcoma Patients' Intense Rehabilitation with Exercise. Paddy, who is a wonderful person, does a lot of work with amputees and with knee replacement patients. She's an amputee herself, so she really understands what it's like. She once had a group of athletes who competed in the Paralympics. I was supposed to start working with her after my surgery and some preliminary physical therapy but it hasn't worked out. The problem is, every time I feel good enough for physical therapy, they figure I'm strong enough to get hit with another chemo. It's a really vicious circle. I have gone over to talk to her several times about her swimming group, and she's shown me the therapy room. She's given me a few exercises that I should do to strengthen both my legs while I'm waiting. She told me that when you're in the hospital it's too easy to sit on your duff doing nothing.

Having cancer is definitely tough. But I'm learning to deal with it and that's something that's taken a long time — over a year. Now I realize I have to stick it out despite the discomfort, especially when you know people who have finished treatment, successfully. When I started treatment, many of the people I met at the hospital were half-way through treatment. Now most of them are well and I'm halfway there. At first I wasn't sure that I'd make it. Now I believe that if they survived, I can, too!

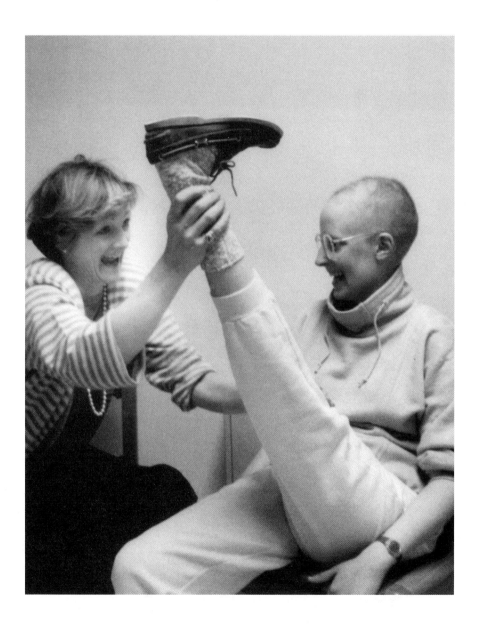

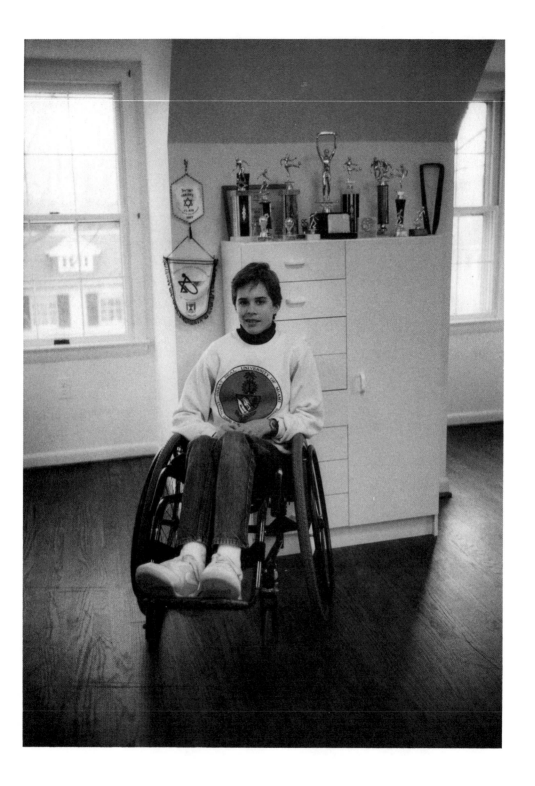

RYAN
MARTIN

AGE FOURTEEN

Spinal Cord Injury

I was twelve and a half when it happened. It was in January and we were coming home from dinner at my little brother's school. As we pulled into our parking space, this guy pulled up next to us with his lights out. All of a sudden he hopped out of the car and started shooting at my stepfather. He missed my stepfather but he didn't miss me. The man shooting was the ex-boyfriend of a woman who used to be our housekeeper. He had visited our house lots of times when they were seeing each other, so I recognized him right away. But I hadn't seen him for a while because they had broken up and our housekeeper had stopped working for us. He had been calling our house a lot after she left and my dad had called the police to get him to stop bothering us. When I first saw him that night everything happened so fast I didn't know what to think. I remember begging him not to hurt me and the next thing I knew I was lying on the ground.

I didn't have any pain right after I was shot, even in my back, where one of the two bullets that hit me severed my spinal cord. The first thing I said was that I couldn't feel my legs. My mom said, "You're okay, you're just in shock," but I knew that something serious had happened to me. I was lying on the ground thinking, "It's going to snow. How am I going to get inside?" I felt out of breath, because one lung had collapsed. I had to concentrate on breathing, because it was so hard. As soon as the ambulance came they gave me oxygen.

83

They took me to Children's Hospital National Medical Center in Washington, D.C., and I stayed there for six weeks. It was a life-or-death situation for the first twenty-four hours. The first thing I remember is waking up inside a big machine where I was having a CAT scan. I wasn't in pain but I felt uncomfortable. I had been in there for five hours. I kept dozing off and then waking up. I don't remember much after that, besides lying in bed in the intensive care unit. I couldn't move much at all, so I would just sort of turn my eyes and watch the heart monitor.

I had tubes going into my side. These were really uncomfortable, especially when the doctors pulled them out after several weeks. It was scary, then painful. My mom tells me that there was a lot of pain in the first two weeks but I don't really remember this too well. I was so drugged that I don't actually remember the moment when my parents told me that I would never be able to walk again. Maybe that's because it's something I already knew when I was lying on the ground. Anyway, I was definitely not thinking about the future. I was still too confused about what was happening on a moment-to-moment basis. I know that I was very sore and achy for a long time. I still feel some tingling in my legs sometimes — "phantom pain." The doctors told me that when a person is paralyzed or loses a limb, it is normal to imagine that he or she still has feeling in that place.

Our friends and family helped us through the whole trauma. They were just great while I was at Children's. They took care of the house when my parents were out, made food, and arranged stuff. I had a million visitors, too. My room had hundreds of cards all over the walls and I had around twenty balloons and tons of chocolate and gum in the room every day. I also became very close to my science teacher, Dave Jacobs, after it happened. He's not like a teacher — he's more like a best friend. He slept at the hospital to relieve my parents and he visited me during the day when he finished teaching. My parents slept there, too, and were with me around the clock. This support definitely made it easier for me.

Another thing that helped my recovery was knowing that I didn't have to worry that the man who shot me would come after me again. He committed suicide. If he hadn't done that, I would have always been on edge. I also think I was lucky that I didn't have to deal with a trial. I would have had to see him again, which I didn't want to do, and all my anger and fear would have taken energy that I needed to concentrate on getting better.

After I got out of Children's, I went to the Alfred I. du Pont Institute in Wilmington, Delaware, a rehabilitation hospital for kids that is a two-and-a-half-hour car ride from our house. I stayed there for three months. At first, my parents came to visit me on weekends and I had quite a few visitors. Later, my family and friends brought me home every weekend.

At du Pont, they had me swimming every day. I had physical therapy, occupational therapy, bowling, Ping-Pong, and basketball, not to mention schoolwork. I also saw a psychiatrist once or twice a week. I was busy until six o'clock every night, and at six there was a place you could go to do artwork or listen to music or watch TV. We had TVs in our rooms, too. It was a good setup there.

In some ways, I was the healthiest person at du Pont — the first person to want to keep going and not to stop. I think seeing how well off I was compared with some of the other kids there probably helped me recover emotionally in a short time. Another thing that helped a lot was not thinking about the future very much. I never worried much about anything. All I was concentrating on was learning new ways to move my body, which is paralyzed from the waist down.

A short time after I left du Pont, we moved into a new house. It wasn't so much that I wanted to get away from our old house, where the shooting happened, but more that the new house has an elevator, which means I can get around more easily. We also have stairs, which I use mostly for therapy. Once a week, with the help of my physical therapist, I put on leg braces and go up all three flights backwards, using my crutches to lift my body up each step. This strengthens my arms and upper body and has helped me a lot. It also keeps my legs in a standing position, which is good for my whole body. There are some nasty hills to get over in Washington, especially when you're in a wheelchair, but the stronger I get, the easier it is to move around.

I don't remember a lot about learning to use a wheelchair. One of the hardest things to master was going over curbs. You have to take a running start and push the back wheels up very hard. But getting around is not a big deal at all. My street wheelchair has handles so that people can pull me upstairs. My sports wheelchair is fast and light, so playing tennis isn't as difficult as it looks.

It was at du Pont that I started going around in sports wheelchairs. When they showed me my first one, I was thrilled. I thought it was so neat! First I started playing sports like basketball. Soon after that I decided that I wanted to try to learn tennis. That first summer out of the hospital, I joined a tennis team coached by Paul Penniman, my school coach. He didn't know anything about wheelchairs, and we were both somewhat nervous when I started taking lessons, but then we began to work it out. Now I'm playing against adults and juniors. As far as I know, I'm the only wheelchair player on the East Coast in national competition who's only fourteen. On the West Coast there is much more junior competition. I've obviously gotten a lot of attention, being able to start on the tennis circuit about ten years earlier than most people would and being sent to tournaments with the help of sponsors.

Last year, for example, my mom and I went to Israel. The U.S. Committee, Sports for Israel, asked me if I'd like to go to the Israel Sports Center, a sports center for disabled athletes. I said I'd love to, since I had been to Israel before and had liked it a lot. The center gives disabled kids an opportunity to be proud athletes. There's nothing like it in the United States. I had a great time there and I made friends. I didn't play any matches there, but I played a lot of practice games with world-class Israeli champions. I'd love to go back.

I think my little brother envies me for getting a lot of attention and going to Israel more than I envy him for being able to run around. He's been through a lot, especially for a four-year-old. He didn't see me, except for a few hours at a time, for about six months. He was, of course, wondering where I was and what was going on. He didn't even know what a hospital was, but he knew that it wasn't a good place to be. It was tough on him because my mom couldn't concentrate on him. He's had it rough, but he's done great.

Before the shooting, I was on the soccer and basketball teams at my school. They said I was the leader of the soccer team. I think what I miss most now is the excitement of playing in those games with my friends. I can still play basketball, but it's a much bigger deal for me to play in a basketball game now that we have to round up an entire team of wheelchair players. Mainly I do individual sports such as singles and doubles competitive tennis, snow skiing, table tennis, and some swimming.

Recently, I played tennis doubles with a quadriplegic who has some use of his arms. He has to have a plastic mold of his hand around the racquet because he can't really hold it, but he's ranked number six in the United States in his division. He's not quick, but he's got a great backhand and a good forehand. I hope I can play with him again soon.

I guess I have bad days, but my friends and family give me a lot of emotional support when I get down. Physically, I don't need too much from them, except to be driven around. I can't drive myself yet. I take the subway to school and around Washington. Sometimes it kind of bothers me when people ask me if I need help. They think I'm helpless. I really don't need any help unless I ask for it.

Once in a while I dream that I'm in a wheelchair and then I get out and start walking around. In my dream I ask, "What do I need this wheelchair for?" and I throw the wheelchair away. When I wake up in the morning I don't know what's going on. It's weird and it confuses me.

The Miami Project is a group doing research to cure paralysis. They are trying to find ways for paralyzed people to relearn to walk. They are also researching methods of rejoining injured nerves. If they can do it, I'd like to be one of the first people they try it on. In the meantime, I don't think of myself as handicapped because that seems like a bigger deal than what's happened to me. If people stare or ask questions, I say I'm in a wheelchair. If I were to meet other kids who were in a similar situation to mine, I'd tell them sports are mental as well as physical. I'd say, "Why not play basketball or tennis? Whatever you want to do, you can do."

ALISHA WEISSMAN

Epilepsy

I was diagnosed as having epilepsy in March 1988, but it turns out I had the disease for about two years before that. What I had at first is called petit mal, and it's the milder type of epileptic seizure. Mild and severe epileptic seizures occur when abnormal electrical impulses go through the brain and send warning signals to other parts of the body, which produce uncontrolled movements. About one in every two hundred people has epilepsy.

The symptoms of petit mal are what I call "blank-outs." It was almost as if I would nod off for a second or two. I would stare and I couldn't hear what people were saying. I would stop talking in mid-sentence. Sometimes I would drop whatever I was holding in my hands.

For a long time I didn't take the petit mal seriously. I only had one or two blank-outs a week at first, and they were usually related to how much sleep I was getting. I figured they were caused by nerves and late nights staying up studying. I also thought that maybe they were part of adolescence, a piece of puberty.

Around January 1988, the petit mal seizures got much worse. I would have as many as five blank-outs in a two-minute period. It became difficult for me to differentiate between what was real and what was a dream. Also, my right arm started to twitch. If I had to speak in front of my class, I'd be afraid I was going to lose my train of thought.

My schoolwork was affected because I couldn't concentrate or remember what was going on in class. Still, strange as it may seem, I never went to see a doctor. My parents had recently gotten divorced and I thought maybe I was spaced out partly due to this.

The morning I had my first grand mal seizure, I was supposed to go to a softball convention in Maryland. Even though I was only a freshman, I had made the varsity team and was chosen with some other kids to represent my school. As I was getting ready to leave my apartment, I had three blank-outs in the time span of a minute. Each time I blanked out, my arm would twitch.

I went down in the elevator to meet my friend in front of the building and suddenly got this strange feeling in my left arm. The feeling traveled across my body to my other arm, which had risen by itself, above my head. I found myself staring up at the palm of my right hand. Then I lost control of my body and felt myself having a seizure. I remember thinking this had to be related to the blank-outs. And that was it. Everything went black.

When the elevator got to the lobby, the doorman went crazy. He thought I was drunk and had passed out. He called up to my father's apartment and sent me right back up. I was kicking so hard I knocked my father over when he tried to get me out of the elevator. He finally got me into the apartment and called 911, which is the police emergency number. I was lying on the foyer floor unconscious for fifteen minutes after that because seizures leave you totally wiped out.

The police showed up before the ambulance because there was an ambulance strike. My father was worried about that because they didn't know what to do. A friend of my father's wife told us to go to Lenox Hill Hospital. The first thing they did at the hospital was to take blood. I have very tiny veins so they couldn't get it out of my arm. Two interns tried and then the chief resident. He was finally able to do it by using a vein in the back of my hand. Now I know what it feels like to get blood taken out from between your knuckles. The whole thing was really scary. I finally broke down and cried while my father was filling out my admission papers.

I stayed in the hospital for three days while they got the results of my CAT scan and electroencephalogram. For the CAT scan, they injected dye into my blood. I was in a lot of pain — it made me feel all hot inside. It was a horrible experience, but it's the only way they can look at the anatomy of the brain. The doctors wanted to be sure that my seizures weren't being caused by a brain tumor. They also did an electroencephalogram. Electrodes attached to my head measured my brain waves. The pattern of my brain waves showed that I have a classic case of epilepsy.

Being in the hospital was awful. My tongue was all bitten up so I couldn't eat. They had to put an IV into the back of my hand, and I kept knocking it against the bed rail. The only good part of my stay was the second day, when I walked into the waiting room and saw thirty of my friends who had come to visit me. My coach was there, too. I couldn't believe my eyes when I saw them. I didn't even think I knew that many people who cared about me. It meant a lot.

While I was in the hospital, a pediatric neurologist, Dr. Kaufman, was called in to evaluate my case. He put me on Depakote, which is an anticonvulsant drug. When I started on Depakote, I took 250

milligrams in the morning and 250 at night. Now that my body has built up a tolerance to the drug I'm up to 1,000 milligrams. Every day I take a 250 and a 125 pill in the morning, a 250 in the afternoon, and a 250 and a 125 again at night. I'm responsible for remembering to take my pills every day. I bring them to school with me in a pillbox. I have to have my blood tested every few months so that Dr. Kaufman can make sure that my medication level is high enough.

Depakote is okay because unlike some other epilepsy medications, it doesn't cause acne. At first it made me feel sick and I had some short-term memory loss, but I'm used to it now and just ignore it and roll with the punches. The pills do make me moody and tired, though. I get so exhausted it's unbelievable and my mood swings are weird. Sometimes I'll be a complete bitch to everyone and not think anything of it. Still, between the tiredness and the mood swings, I somehow get my work done and stay active in sports. Things are actually a lot easier for me now that I can concentrate on what's happening in school and everywhere else.

I'm lucky because I have friends who understand my condition. At first, though, it was hard to know what to say to them. How do you tell your friends you're an epileptic? You can't just say, "I have epilepsy, can you pass the milk?" Actually, I knew they would take it fine, even though they'd be a bit surprised. I'm very athletic and I worried that it might be hard for them to realize that someone who is as active as I am could have a disease. I guess it's true that bad things can happen to anyone.

As it turns out, it was fortunate for me that my schoolmates knew all about my problem. Six weeks later I was at my friend Mark's apartment when I had my second grand mal seizure. It didn't last as long this time. We were about to go to a café downtown with some other friends when I suddenly fell on the floor. Mark called 911, the ambulance came, and they all went with me to the Lenox Hill Emergency Room. My parents were both away so my friends had to take care of everything. They were great!

When I got to the hospital this time the doctors had the same old problem drawing blood. They finally did it after three tries. I kept telling them to take it from between my knuckles but they didn't want to listen. When they finally paid attention to me they succeeded. I felt cold and exhausted, the same as when I had my first seizure, but we decided to get a second opinion. Dr. Gold, another pediatric neurologist, examined me and then he and Dr. Kaufman discussed my case. They decided that I needed to kick up my medication. We did and I haven't had a grand mal since. I haven't had a petit mal since July 5, 1988.

I'm really happy about this. My greatest fear when I found out I had epilepsy was that I wouldn't be able to lead a normal life. For example, I didn't think I'd be able to continue with sports. I love sports. I play volleyball in the fall, basketball in the winter, and softball in the

spring. If I weren't able to keep active this way I'd go crazy. It's a great outlet for me, especially now that I have to deal with mood swings. My other greatest fear was that I wouldn't be able to get my driver's license. But it turns out that won't be a problem either because I can apply for one as soon as I've been seizure-free for one year.

Being an athlete has definitely helped me deal with epilepsy. I'd say the most important thing that athletics has taught me is to watch out for myself and not overdo whatever I'm doing. I've learned how to take care of my body, which includes being responsible about my behavior. For example, one weekend shortly after my first grand mal, I went drinking with some friends. We all went out to shoot pool and have a few beers. Well, that's the sort of thing I'm not doing again because I think that drinking while taking my medication definitely lowered the effectiveness of it. Now that I don't drink anymore, I'm the one who puts my friends in cabs or brings them home to my house to make sure they're okay. Much to my own surprise, I've found I can have a fine time without drinking or doing drugs and I definitely feel better.

All in all, my life hasn't changed that much as a result of having epilepsy. The only thing I can't do is scuba dive because if I had a seizure under water I could drown. I take a few simple precautions such as not locking the bathroom door in case I need help, wearing my Medic Alert bracelet at all times, and never swimming alone. I do have to go and see Dr. Kaufman every three months so he can do a blood test and make sure I'm doing well. He's the only doctor who has ever been able to draw blood without killing me. I'm doing my biology research paper on epilepsy so on my last visit I interviewed him about my own case. He showed me the printout of my brain waves and gave me some brochures.

My parents have both been really supportive these past few years. My mother always reminds me that Napoleon and Julius Caesar both had

epilepsy and they conquered half the world . . . without Depakote. Right now I'm just concentrating on playing sports and learning how to drive. That's good enough for me!

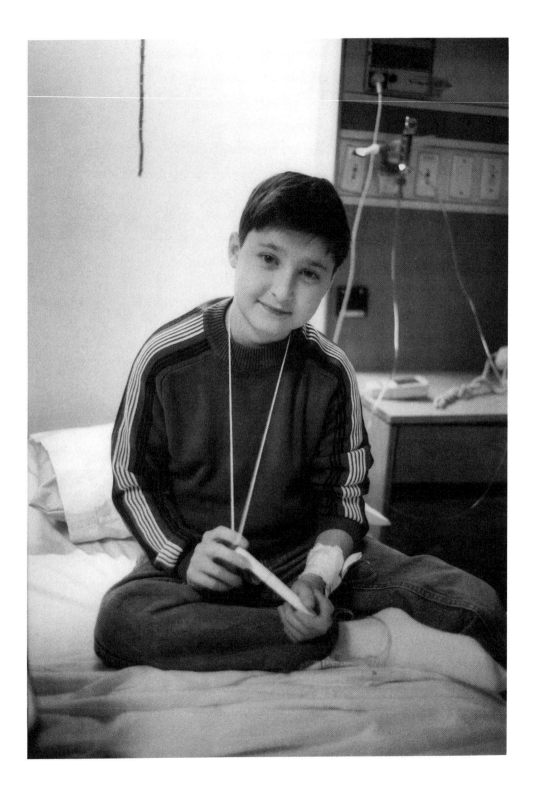

JIMMY
O'NEILL

AGE FIFTEEN

Cystic Fibrosis

I was born with cystic fibrosis. It was diagnosed when I was only one day old. It's a hereditary recessive lung disease. Both parents have to carry the genes in order for you to inherit it. I have a younger brother, Andrew, who's twelve and he's OK. If you're not born with it you can't get it later on.

I didn't start having any lung problems until I was about six. That was the first time I came to the hospital and I've been hospitalized thirty to thirty-five times since then. I get admitted five to six times a year and I usually stay five to ten days each time. I always come to the same hospital, which helps because now I know all the nurses in the unit and it's like a second home. My family moved here from Michigan and my dad got a new job so I would have this advantage.

When I come into the hospital it's for one of two reasons. Sometimes I come in because I have a cold and I need to get hooked up to an IV with antibiotics to help me fight off the infection. Other times I feel a little sick and I come in for what they call a tune-up. My body is sort of like a car that everyone wants to keep in tip-top shape.

For the most part I decide when I need to get tuned up. It's when I'm not feeling well, I'm cranky, and I can't sleep much. Sometimes my family is the first to notice. They know me better than anyone and can tell by my mood swings. If anything good has come out of having this disease, it's that it has brought our family closer together. It's made our relationship better and strengthened our ties because we have to depend on one another.

It's hard to explain how it feels to have cystic fibrosis. Because I've had it all my life I don't know how it feels *not* to have it. But the way I feel could be how a normal person feels when he has a cold — what you would call congested. There are other times when I don't feel good at all but can't say why.

When I'm at home I have to follow a daily routine that consists of medication and physical therapy. I'm responsible for the medication and I take about twenty-five pills a day. When I'm in school the nurse keeps them for me in her office and I go in between classes to get them. I also leave an inhaler in there so if I need to I can pop in and take two puffs.

My mom and dad take turns doing the physical therapy. When I'm in the hospital, it's often done by Katherine Parker, who is one of my physical therapists. It's called chest P.T. and it takes about twenty minutes. Some people call it "thumping." It's basically hitting me on the back to bring up the mucus that gets congested in my chest. It makes me cough, which is good for me. When I start coughing it can sound horrible but it helps me feel better. I'm lucky that I've been in the same school for a long time because my classmates know me and accept it. But when you're younger or new at school, I can see how it would be a problem.

When I first started in my school we had to explain to many people that what I had wasn't catching. By now most of my friends know what I've got and how it affects me, so they overlook it and treat me normally — as normally as possible. I say that because I can't live a totally normal life. For example, I can't play sports. It's hard for me because I'm personally very competitive and I like that kind of stuff. When I was younger, before the disease got worse, I could do more.

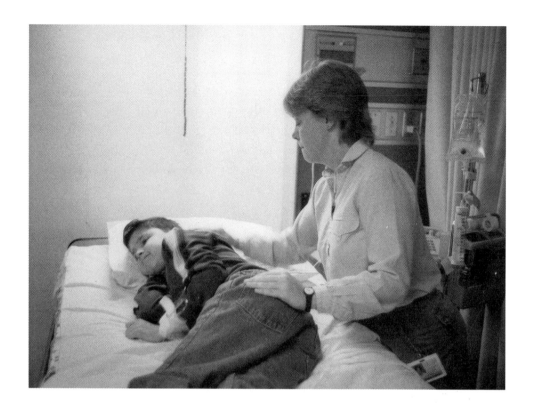

But now I get too short of breath. At least I'm old enough to realize that maybe it's not my purpose in life to play sports. I suppose I'm lucky because everything else I want to do is pretty much within my reach and I'm able to see that life goes on. I know there are some things I'll be able to do and some things I won't.

Since I have to have my physical therapy like clockwork twice a day, it does put a limit on the things I can do. I can go to my friends' houses for sleepovers, but because of my medication schedule it's not worth the inconvenience. And I don't like to go away for club trips for the same reason. It's easier to go to special sleep-away camps. A couple of years ago I went to a cystic fibrosis camp in Michigan where they provide special treatment. I'd like to be able to go to a regular camp but no one wants the responsibility. A lot of people are just plain ignorant and afraid of any kind of risk. People read a pamphlet that was put out fifteen years ago and think that if you cough you're going to die on them.

In a way, the most difficult aspect of this disease emotionally, for me, is to have to depend so much on other people to do things for me. I'm at an age where most of my friends are gaining more and more independence. I have to realize that no matter what, I'll never be totally independent. There's always going to have to be someone there for me. And yet, I'm probably much older in a lot of ways than some of my friends because of all I've been though. There's definitely an advantage to seeing life in the real world firsthand the way I have. I've been able to see at an early age that there's more to life than just going to school and being in your own little clique. Some of my classmates never go outside of their own small group for anything and it limits them. There's a whole other life out there where you're not always going to be surrounded and protected by a group of friends.

I'm definitely planning to go to college when I graduate from high school. My dad and I have gone to a workshop sponsored by the Cystic Fibrosis Foundation and we're looking at a lot of brochures. I'm hoping to find something that's about three hours away. That would mean I'd have a sense of independence, which I need, but that I'd be close enough to come home if there was a medical emergency.

I hope I'll get married when I'm older but I realize that having children might be a problem. First of all, because I carry a recessive gene, I wouldn't want to pass it on. And also, there could be a physical problem as well, since having cystic fibrosis usually means having a low sperm count. But that all seems so far in the future that I can't say it's something I spend much time thinking about. Mainly I want to be healthy enough to do well in school and my immediate goal is to go away to college.

I never feel jealous of people who aren't sick but I do feel angry when I see healthy people smoking. It makes me mad because they have good lungs and they're ruining them when there are people like me who don't have a choice. Another thing that bothers me is when I see kids trying to skip school as much as they can while someone like me has to miss fifty to sixty days a year! People don't realize what they have and then they go ahead and abuse it.

My disease will definitely get worse unless they find some kind of cure. In the meantime, they keep trying different medicines because, as with all diseases, after you've been on a certain medication for a long time, you build up a resistance and the medicine no longer works. With cystic fibrosis, once you get lung damage, you can't repair the damaged part. Your lungs start filling up with junk and it gets harder and harder to breathe. It's like a sink drain that keeps getting clogged up until finally it's so bad you can't do anything about it. It gets progressively worse and you can't do anything to reverse the damage. Finally it gets to the point where you just can't breathe anymore.

There's a lot of talk about heart-lung transplants, but I don't see them as a solution because it would be so temporary. The gene that makes the mucus is in your body system, so even if you get new lungs the gene keeps on going and those new lungs will eventually get all clogged up like the ones I have. Basically, what they have to do is to find some cure that will stop the disease itself.

My life is different from those of other kids but because I've grown up with it, it's something I've gotten used to. It's probably as hard for you to imagine what my life is like as it is for me to imagine how some other people live. I can't see how a stockbroker might get up at three-thirty in the morning and not get home until ten at night. And I can't imagine what it would be like to have diabetes and to give yourself shots. I suppose there are all sorts of people who are *so* used to what they have to do that it doesn't seem weird. It's how they live. I think in some ways I'm better off than some kids who get paralyzed or go blind all of a sudden. It's so much easier if you don't know what you're missing because you've never had it to begin with.

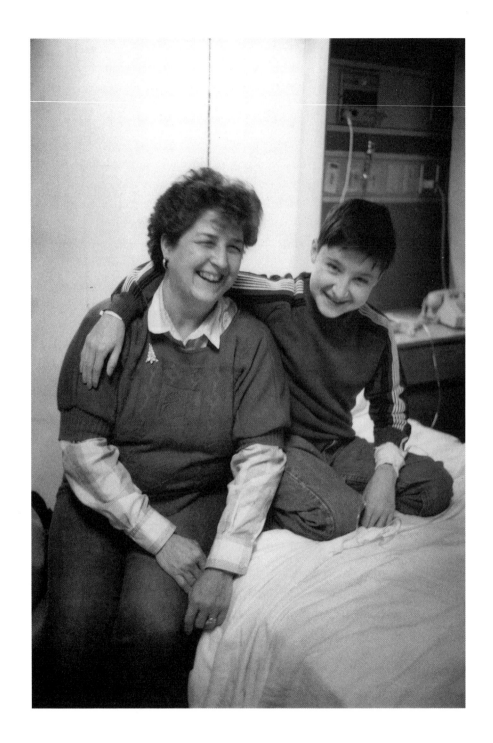

I go to church once a week, which is a source of comfort for me. Mostly I pray that God will take care of me, no matter what happens. There are some things in life you have choices about and there are things you don't. Having cystic fibrosis is one of those things where there isn't a whole lot I can do, other than praying and having faith that everything will be taken care of. You always have to have a little hope because if you run out of that there's nothing worth anything. You might as well give up right then and there.

There is one big advantage in believing in God, which is that I believe there is a heaven and hell based on what Jesus says in the Bible. And I am certain that when I die it's going to be a big relief because I am never going to have to worry about pain again.

I have faith that there is a reason I have this disease. God didn't just draw my name out of a hat. There has to be a reason why I'm sick, why I have the wonderful parents and brother I have, and I have faith that God will take care of whatever is going to happen. Sometimes I think that maybe he knew I'd have this attitude and he put me here so other kids who are sick can see me and say, "Hey, you know, maybe he's right, maybe there *is* hope." I'd like to think that. Or maybe I've talked to somebody in a way that helped them get through a hard time. I like to feel that when people see me they realize their own lives could be a lot worse and maybe they appreciate how lucky they are. That's what often happens to me. I look at some of the other kids on the ward, or I read about small children starving in Ethiopia, and I realize how lucky *I* am!

SPENCER GRAY

AGE SIXTEEN

Kidney Disease

My kidneys failed when I was eleven years old. I was at school one day and I didn't feel too good. My hands and feet were cramped and I couldn't walk. My father was at work, but my mother just happened to be home that day. She took me to the emergency room at the Children's Hospital National Medical Center in Washington, D.C.

In the hospital they started doing a lot of tests and stuck an IV in me. I was never scared of needles before, but this time I was scared — they were sticking a whole bunch of needles into me. When they finished their tests, they told me I had kidney disease.

I stayed in the hospital for two weeks, and then I was allowed to go back to school. The doctors told me that I needed a transplant, but in the meantime, in a month's time, I would have to start hemodialysis. That's where they pump your blood through a machine to clean it, since your kidneys can't do the work they are supposed to do by themselves. To get me ready for dialysis, they tied a vein and an artery together in my arm and made a fistula, so that blood could flow from my veins into the machine more easily. A fistula looks like a large new vein that is about the diameter of a pencil. If you touch it, you can feel a buzz because the blood is rushing through.

When I went on dialysis, I had to go to the hospital three times a week, for four hours each time. A lot of adults told me that when they started, they were afraid that they wouldn't be able to take it. Once I learned more about it, I thought dialysis wasn't so scary. I think things were easier in the children's unit because I could watch TV, play games, talk — anything I wanted, as long as I didn't get up and walk around. Sometimes they would bring in movies. They even had ones rated PG, not just kid stuff. They provided the food, too. I ate loads of hamburgers. Doing my homework was the most boring part.

At first it was hard keeping up with my schoolwork. They made me come to the hospital early in the morning or in the middle of the school day, at noon. Going back and forth also took a lot of time. I would have preferred going in the evening and being able to go home afterward, because dialysis tires you out. I hardly had any energy at all. People would say, "He's sleeping all the time. How come he's not eating like everybody else?" That's the way it was. I wasn't eating very much and I slept too much. It made me sort of depressed.

My older brother, Sean, was a big help. Whenever I was feeling sad, he would say or do funny things to cheer me up. He was always drawing pictures of me, and whenever he went out, he would take me for a ride with him.

After dialysis you don't feel very well, but if you didn't have it, you'd feel worse. That's how it goes. On dialysis you don't feel great, but you know that when you get your kidney transplant, you'll feel a lot better.

The doctors put my name on a list so that when a kidney became available for transplant, I'd get it. My parents' kidneys matched mine and they would have given me one of theirs, but I didn't want them. Even though the doctors said that with all the new medicines they have nowadays, it was impossible for the person donating to get sick, I didn't want to take the chance that two members of the family would have kidney disease.

It was around this time that the doctors gave me an eye test and saw cystine crystals in them. They told me I had cystinosis, which is a rare disorder that affects most of the major organs in the body. The doctors determined that I was born with this disease and that it was because of this that I had developed kidney failure when I was eleven. Since then my legs have been affected, too. And my eyes. Most times it hurts to walk, and my eyes are very sensitive to sunlight and lights.

After I had been on dialysis for about four months the doctors told me to just stay at the hospital after one of my treatments. I wanted to go home, so it made me angry but then they told me they had found a kidney donor for me. That was on Friday, March 2, 1984.

Next, they put me on a new drug called cyclosporine. It's a liquid medicine and it tastes horrible. It was OK, though, because they mixed it with chocolate milk. When I got used to it, I could take it straight.

CBS Television was in the process of gathering information for a documentary they were about to do on transplants and had been interviewing me while I was on dialysis. When they found out I was about to get a transplant, they taped my entire surgery. There were cameras all over the place. But I tried my best to ignore them. I was worried about the transplant, which is a major operation. Later, when I went into the operating room, I was so nervous that I didn't even see the cameras. The one-hour program was shown on national television. My uncle was stationed in Germany at the time and he called us that night to say they saw it.

The nurses took me into a little room to prepare me for surgery. My mother was there for a while but left just before they put me to sleep. They put me to sleep about an hour before the operation, and I don't think I woke up for almost a day. The doctors told me the operation was five and a half hours long, but all I remember is waking up in the recovery room. About thirteen hours after the operation, they moved me to intensive care.

I was in the ICU for about two days. There was a lot of pain, but I felt better than I had before the transplant. I knew I had a new kidney because I felt like I was clean. You can tell when something is working inside you — you feel different. I felt great.

Doctors think they know how kids feel when they are going through things like this, but it's not true. I thought I could tell how a medicine was going to work the first time I took it, but the doctors didn't believe me. They go by the book, and they don't know everything. My doctors were all great but the nurses were much nicer. They were more emotional, seemed to care more. When a kid was sick, they got sad. They really looked after us. For example, I like to have my feet rubbed, and they would rub my feet and shoulders whenever I wanted.

After my transplant, I actually had three kidneys inside me — the new one and my old ones. That's because my diseased kidneys were very small and each one was no bigger than a golf ball. Even though they weren't functioning, there weren't any poisons coming out of them so they weren't doing any harm either. To take them out would have required two more hours of major surgery. Unfortunately, seven months later, my body rejected the new kidney and in January 1985 they had to remove it. I had to go back on dialysis and I went back on the list of people who needed a new kidney. I also started getting ready for the next transplant. I was upset to be back on dialysis, but I was thankful that I had been off of it for seven months.

My second transplant was on July 1, 1985. They had put the first kidney in on my left side, and they put the new one in on the right. That one worked for a little over two years but in December 1987, it started showing signs of rejection and I was sick a lot.

Since January 1988 I have been back on dialysis but now I'm on "peritoneal" dialysis, which means I have a solution that cleanses my system. It's a lot more convenient for me than the hemodialysis because I can do it at home instead of having to go to the hospital. I have a permanent tube in my stomach and I hook myself up to my dialysis machine every night when I go to bed. It is really important that I don't get an infection so I have to be very, very careful. We had a two-week training period at the hospital where they taught me that an infection would be painful and dangerous. I have to "scrub down" just like a doctor going into surgery. I wear a mask and rubber gloves for this procedure. My room has to be closed off while I'm sterilizing my stomach with Betadine, which is like iodine except that it doesn't sting, and peroxide. Someone always has to be at home with me while I'm doing this because if I should drop something I have to call for help so I don't contaminate the sterile area on my stomach. My mom usually is my backup. I try to start everything around eight-thirty P.M. so I'm ready to get into bed by nine and go to sleep by ten. Since I have to be hooked up to the machine for ten hours, I get up around seven A.M. I have to be just as careful when I disconnect myself, so I repeat the sterile procedure all over again. I'm so used to doing it now that it's just like brushing my teeth. Then I start getting ready for school.

These past few years have been such an emotional roller coaster for me that I recently decided to take my name off the transplant list. At this point I want to wait and see how I do on dialysis. I'm not sure when I want to try another transplant since I've tried two and neither has worked. Surgery is great when it's successful, but when it's not you get very depressed and frustrated. It's such a tremendous letdown. I miss a lot of school. It's a rough road. Of course, the doctors would say you can't achieve success if you don't keep trying, but then they're not the ones experiencing the pain. Now that I can do my dialysis at home, I'm living a fairly normal life and that's important to me. I have time for elective courses and I also have time to socialize with my friends. If I were hospitalized for another transplant or on hemodialysis, I would have to cut way back on these activities.

I go to the hospital for clinic checkups once a month or, if I have any problems, more often. First, I see my nurse, Gerry Todd, who checks my book. It's like a diary and every day I write down my blood pressure and weight and how I'm feeling. Then the lab people draw blood samples and after they look at the results — we call them my "numbers" — they decide whether I need to make any adjustments in my medication or in my fluid intake.

When I finish with Gerry, I see a bunch of doctors. Then I visit with the nutritionist and with the social worker. Sometimes I have an eye test. Gerry sets this all up in advance to my coming in. He has always taken special care of me — through my good times and bad — ever since I was eleven. He's tops. He even took me to my first football game at the RFK Stadium.

Everybody who has kidney problems has to see a psychiatrist. Doctors tell you to go and talk about any problems you have. I refused to go at first, because I didn't understand what a psychiatrist was. Luckily, I changed my mind and I've been seeing Dr. Hersh for a couple of years. I used to go every Friday, but now I go once every three months or so. Dr. Hersh is very funny, and he's nice — no boring lying on a

couch while he writes stuff. He likes to do things with me. He helped me send away for a poster showing what I am allowed to eat, since I have to eat a lot of salt-free stuff like fruits and vegetables to make sure my blood pressure stays low. Dr. Hersh was especially supportive when we first found out I had cystinosis. Living with kidney failure had been hard enough and I needed a lot of help with it when I learned about this other disease. I was scared!

The National Institutes of Health in Bethesda, Maryland, have been experimenting with a medicine they hope will help slow down the development process of cystinosis, but it's going to be a long time before they know for sure. I was trying it for a while but it tasted like rotten eggs and I couldn't keep it down. It made me throw up and when I did I lost the benefit of the other medicines I was taking.

Before doctors knew a lot about this disease, people who had it lived to be only nineteen or twenty. Now I've met people who are twenty-three or twenty-four years old, and they're doing pretty well. Still, unless they can find a medicine to cure it, I could eventually go blind. In the meantime, between the kidney disease and the cystinosis, I take about twelve different medications every day!

Another major problem caused by cystinosis is that it stunts your growth. I've only grown about two inches since I was nine. This is a big problem for me. It's hard being in high school and looking around and seeing that everybody is twice my size. Also, a boy my age likes to play big, rough sports, like football and basketball. I can't play football or other contact sports because I might damage the catheter in my stomach, and I can't play basketball because I'm too short. Another thing that bothers me is that people I don't know treat me like a little kid instead of a young man.

Junior ROTC — that stands for Reserve Officers' Training Corps — has been the best thing for me. It's the junior Marines, Air Force, Army, and Navy. I wear my own Navy uniform. They had to order a special one for me because of my height. "Master Gunny" Washing-

ton, who works with our group, told me right off to stop worrying about my size and not to think of myself as a novelty. What he said was, "Size doesn't mean anything. It's the size of your heart that matters."

I go to training every day at seven-thirty, and on Tuesdays and Thursdays I have drill at eight o'clock. We've won the city championship for four years in a row. When I go to ROTC, I forget that I'm smaller than the other kids, and a lot of the time I even forget I'm sick. All I feel is real proud.

I am now taking driver's education in school and it's amazing to drive by people and they do a double take — they can't believe I'm driving because of my height. But my instructor says I'm doing great!

I just want to have as normal a life as I can. I have my father, my mother, and my brother, Sean, to thank for always being there for me.

RACHEL
DEMASTER

AGE TEN

Juvenile Diabetes Mellitus

I was seven years old when my mom told me I had diabetes. It was a big shock because other than having to go to the bathroom more than usual I was feeling fine. I had gone to my doctor for a regular checkup and he found sugar in my urine. This was a sign that my pancreas wasn't working right.

When my mother explained to me what diabetes was I burst into tears. I was afraid I was going to die. Even after my parents convinced me that this wasn't going to happen, I felt that my life was going to change completely.

My pancreas is in my tummy and it produces insulin. Insulin helps the body to process sugar and turn it into energy. There are two kinds of diabetes, Type One and Type Two. In Type One the pancreas can't produce insulin at all. In Type Two there's nothing wrong with the pancreas but the cells in the rest of the body don't respond to the insulin. Type One used to be called juvenile onset diabetes because it occurred most frequently among kids, but now they've learned that grown-ups can also get Type One. I have Type One, which means that I have to get insulin shots.

I was really lucky that my pediatrician noticed a problem so quickly because we were able to start treatment right away. I was diagnosed in December and a couple of months later, when it was time for me to start taking insulin, I went to the hospital and stayed there for three days. I was in Mount Sinai Hospital in New York City, which has one of the best diabetes programs anywhere. I wasn't sick when I went in — they just wanted to monitor my reaction to the insulin. It was also the best way for them to educate me and my parents. The doctors gave Mom and Dad a book to study and the diabetes team showed them how to take care of me.

While I was in the hospital, a nurse gave me my injections but they also started teaching my parents how to give me my insulin shots and blood tests. I have to have two shots of insulin every day, one when I get up in the morning and one about a half hour before I eat dinner.

I take two different kinds of insulin, a short-acting one and a long-acting one. The amount of each depends on the results of my blood test. I usually have the same amount of the long-acting one and different amounts of the short-acting one, but this also depends on the season and how much exercise I'm planning to get. Things like getting sick also change my insulin dose. For example, when I have the flu I have to take more because my blood sugar level shoots up.

The first time my mother gave me an insulin shot, I could tell she was really scared. We were both afraid it would hurt. After experimenting with a few different kinds of needles we found one that's so sharp it hardly hurts. Last year I learned to give myself injections. First, I practiced the whole technique on an old doll. In the beginning I was scared that it would hurt more if I did it. Now I'm scared it'll hurt more when my mother does it.

Some people use air guns without a needle for giving insulin. I've heard that the air pressure coming out of the gun hurts as much as getting a needle so I still take injections.

Insulin shots keep the amount of sugar in my blood at the right level but only on a temporary basis. That's why I have to give myself blood

tests to make sure everything is okay. The blood test is more annoying than painful — just a tiny little finger prick. The first time I had to have one I was so scared I hid in my father's closet. I sat there behind his shoes and wouldn't come out. My parents talked to me for a while and finally I agreed to let them do the test. I was so nervous that I think I made it hurt more than it should have. Nowadays I'm so used to it that I can do it in the morning without even getting out of bed. I take turns with my fingers. I never use my thumbs or pinkies. I have callouses on my pointer fingers, middle fingers, and ring fingers because I've stuck myself so many times.

In the nurse's office at school I have a special machine that tests my blood for me. If I'm not feeling well I'll go and have a test. My teacher also checks to make sure that if I'm going to exercise I have some Life Savers or juice with me in case I have a low.

Lows happen when you overdo things that keep your blood sugar low, like taking too much insulin or getting too much exercise. When I get a low I feel shaky and dizzy and blah. Sometimes it gives me a slight headache, too. All I can do is sit. I don't have lows every day but there are days when I have two or three. Usually it depends on how much exercise I'm getting and how the day is going. Sometimes it's hard to distinguish between having a low and feeling crummy. I might go down to the nurse's office and take my blood test and find I'm not low at all.

If I'm having a low and don't do anything for it for a couple of minutes, it won't do any damage. But if I don't get some sugar into my system quickly it can be dangerous. I've never fainted during a low but that's because I always treat it in time. I wear a Medic Alert necklace that tells people I'm an insulin-dependent diabetic. It has phone numbers on it for them to call in case of an emergency. That way, if I'm somewhere alone and I have a problem, people who don't know what's wrong with me will be able to get me help immediately.

My brother, Neil, is great about helping me with my lows. When I'm feeling shaky he'll get me some food so I don't have to get up and move around. He knows that if it's not too bad I should have milk and crackers and that I should drink orange juice if the low is more serious.

For me, the worst part of having diabetes is not being able to eat whatever I want. Unless I'm having a low I can't eat any sugar except the natural type that's in fruit. The sugar that's in candy and cake makes my blood sugar level very high for a long time after I eat it. Once in a while, on special occasions like my birthday, I have cake, but I'm basically not supposed to eat sweets. I feel bad when all my friends are eating candy and I can't have any. Neil is very considerate about not eating candy or cookies in front of me. He's older than I am and if he wants to eat sweets he usually waits until after I've gone to bed. There's one good thing about not eating sugar, which is that I don't have any cavities! My dentist is really proud of me.

On Halloween, my parents and I go trick or treating like everyone else, but since I can't eat the candy my parents buy it from me. They give me five cents for every piece of candy I get and I buy myself a stuffed animal. I have a great collection now. Neil used to eat all of my candy but since he got braces my parents have been buying his candy too.

I would have to say that I miss maple syrup the most of all the things I'm not allowed to eat. I go to the supermarket with my mother and help her with the shopping. We get stuff like diet soda and sugar-free hot chocolate so I don't miss sweet things too much. We spend a long time reading the labels on everything. It's amazing how many foods that don't taste sweet actually have sugar in them.

The worst thing about my diet is that I have to eat so much! Besides breakfast, lunch, and dinner, I have three snacks every day. People with diabetes have to eat a certain amount of carbohydrates and more

protein than most people. This is a pain because I'm not a big eater and especially because I don't like protein. The morning snack we have at school is at just the right time for my first snack of the day. I always have milk and a carbohydrate. When I get home at three-thirty my mom gives me chips or crackers. I like Goldfish a lot because they come in lots of flavors. I'm allowed to eat ice cream because it doesn't have that much sugar and it has fat and protein to balance the sugar, so that's what I have for my evening snack. In the morning, after I get my insulin shot, my mother asks me what I want for breakfast. I usually say, "Pig's feet, please." But I end up eating mozzarella cheese or eggs with toast, fruit, and milk. For lunch, I like to have some peanut butter to take care of the protein. And for dinner I have to eat a protein, a starch, a vegetable, a fruit, and a glass of milk. Our family eats together and we all eat the same food.

I have to be extremely punctual about my meals and snacks so that the food can interact with the insulin properly. This means that my parents always make sure I have food and juice with me when we're on a trip in case we get stuck in traffic. I can never sleep late, even on weekends and holidays, because I have to have my blood tested and take my insulin the first thing in the morning. I also have to eat half an hour after my insulin shot.

Exercise is good for everybody but it's especially good for me. This is because if my blood sugar is high I can lower it by exercising instead of taking insulin. When I want to exercise, I tell my mother in advance and she gives me a smaller dose of insulin. I'm one of the most athletic girls in my class and I've won trophies for swimming and soccer. There are lots of famous athletes who have diabetes. The ones I know about are Bill Talbert and Ham Richardson, who are both great tennis players. Curt Fraser plays hockey for the Minnesota North Stars. My favorite exercise is jogging with my father. We go to the park near our house and we have a great time together.

Besides my regular pediatrician, I see a special doctor for my diabetes every three months. Her name is Dr. Fredda Ginsberg and she's at

Mount Sinai Hospital. People come from all over the world to see her because she's so good. She asks me how much I've been exercising and whether I've been having lots of lows. I also have to have some blood tests when I see her. She lets me take my own blood pressure, which is fun. Dr. Ginsberg is much more than my doctor. She's my friend. I made her a paperweight out of rocks and shells and I crocheted her a little triangle that she pinned on her wall.

Having diabetes hasn't changed my relationships with my friends. However, when I go to play at other people's houses, I usually don't stay for dinner. If I sleep over at a neighbor's house my mom will come over and give me my shot. One time I went to my friend's house and did all my shots myself. Mom gave me instructions about how much insulin I should take so it wasn't hard at all.

Sometimes my friends from school watch to see how I do my blood tests. My brother's friend Mike always covers his eyes and yells "Mommy!" when I stick myself. My friend Dana, who wants to be a scientist when he grows up, likes to keep track of my blood sugar level so that he can tell me how I'm doing.

I have only one friend with diabetes. Her name is Tory and she's nine years old. Dr. Ginsberg introduced us at the hospital and we go to each other's house. If Tory hadn't taken a blood test with me, I never would have thought she had diabetes. She seems very healthy and she doesn't talk about it very much. I don't like to talk about diabetes either but I do like to know all about it. My family subscribes to a magazine called *Forecast,* which has all the latest news about machines and shots and what's going on medically. The best thing about *Forecast* is the section called "Making Friends." You can write to other people with diabetes. It has separate sections for people of all different ages and there's one section called "Friendly People 12 and Under." I think it would be fun to have a pen pal.

I also think it would be fun to go away to a special sleep-away camp for kids with diabetes. I can't go this year because my parents say I'm not old enough but I hope I can next year.

Sometimes I wonder if when I grow up anyone will want to marry me because my children may have diabetes. I worry that it's hereditary because my grandfather had it. My mother told me that it wouldn't be a problem because when people are really in love, the relationship comes first. My brother says that I shouldn't even be thinking about marriage for another fifteen years. He's right! Besides, by then there may be a cure for diabetes. In the meantime, things are okay because no matter what happens, I'm still me.

Acknowledgments

I would not have been able to do this book without the help of many people and I want to thank all of them. My work began in New York, where I live, and it was my good fortune to turn first to Ellen Schwarzman, a tireless member of the board at the Mount Sinai Medical Center. She put me in touch with Dr. Kurt Hirschhorn, Chairman of Pediatrics at Mount Sinai, to whom this book is dedicated. For more than two years this brilliant and compassionate doctor has been available and helpful to me — encouraging and wise. He introduced to me many of his remarkable colleagues: Dr. Richard Golinko, Director of Pediatric Cardiology, Dr. Jeffrey M. Lipton, Director of Pediatric Hematology and Oncology, and Dr. Fredda Ginsberg, Director of Pediatric Endocrinology and Metabolism. Dr. David Kaufman, a pediatric neurologist, also associated with Mount Sinai, appears in this book with Alisha Weissman. I actually tracked him down by myself. That's because his daughter Jill was featured in one of my previous books, *The Fun of Cooking,* where she shares her secrets for perfect Matzo Ball Soup. Other people at Mount Sinai who were helpful include Delores Gray, Nancy Cincotta, M.S.W., and Mary Collins-Pest, R.N.

Another major resource for me was Children's Hospital National Medical Center in Washington, D.C., thanks to Sally Quinn. Sally, who is a friend of mine, is also a member of the Board of Directors. She has been deeply involved with this hospital since the birth of her son, Quinn Bradlee, who, because of a congenital heart problem, has been cared for by the compassionate and competent staff of this remarkable hospital. Sally put me in the capable hands of Beverly Wyckoff Jackson, Assistant Vice President for Public Affairs. They are lucky to have her and I was fortunate to have had her invaluable assistance and warm friendship. I am also grateful to Mary Carroll Sullivan, Manager of Broadcast Services in Public Affairs.

It is at this same hospital that Lynn Ingersoll, M.L.S., Family Librarian, oversees what may be the best hospital library I've ever seen. It is my hope that more and more young patients and their families will avail themselves of these wonderful facilities, not only at this hospital but in hospitals throughout the country. It has been sad for me to spend two years walking down hospital corridors and to have seen so many children staring at TV sets. We need to encourage these youngsters to read more. A hospital bed is an excellent place to exercise one's brain.

Another invaluable source for me in Washington was Dr. Stephen P. Hersh, Co-Director of the Medical Illness Counseling Center. Originally trained in pediatrics, he now devotes his life to helping children and their families deal with the emotional burdens of traumatic injuries and serious chronic illnesses. He is pictured in this book with Spencer Gray. It is my fervent wish that more qualified professionals will enter into this much needed field of work. Steve Hersh, along with Kurt Hirschhorn, was always there for me, holding my hand, guiding me, answering questions and encouraging me to keep on going.

Special thanks too, to my dear friend Phyllis Theroux, with whom I often stayed while in Washington. In addition to her hospitality, she often drove to and from my many interviews.

Bettye Topps, the principal of McKinley High School where Spencer Gray is a student, was warm and friendly. So were "Master Gunny" Charles Washington and "Chief" James Savage, who run the school's ROTC program. Spencer's colleagues in ROTC also deserve special recognition. They are Thomas Rhodes, Rhayne Gadson, Ainsley Brooks, Terence Brown, Bridgette Haythe, Delois Kenny, Norman Queen, and Heather Maxwell. I would also like to express my appreciation to Spencer's nurse, Gerry Todd, for his help.

The Association for the Care of Children's Health is located in Washington, D.C. The address is 3615 Wisconsin Avenue N.W., Washington, D.C. 20016. Beverley H. Johnson is the Executive Director of this wonderful organization dedicated to humanizing health care for children and their families. They have excellent materials and bibliographies related to childhood health and illness.

My association with Memorial Sloan-Kettering Cancer Center goes back to 1978 when I first met Dr. Norma Wollner, Director of the Pediatric Day Hospital, in conjunction with some photographic work I was doing for that outstanding institution. We have remained friends since that time and she was the one who arranged for me to interview Adam Rojo and Elizabeth Bonwich. Dr. Paul A. Marks, Joan Marks, Dr. Richard A. Rifkind, Dr. Paul A. Myers, Dr. William Cahan, Noreen McGowan, R.N., Karrie Zampini, C.S.W., Karin Mullin, Özlem Yavasca, Felicia Dickman, Paddy Rossbach, R.N., Joe Kerest, Bette-Ann Gwathmey, Roseann Ieraci, and Marie Donahue all lent a helping hand. I am especially indebted to Suzanne Rauffenbart, Vice President for Public Affairs at MSK, who has become a good friend.

At Philadelphia Children's Hospital and Philadelphia Children's Seashore House, Dr. Andrew Eichenfield, formerly chief pediatric resident for Dr. Hirschhorn at Mount Sinai, arranged interviews with Marycely Martinez and Lauren Dutton. Patty Rettig, R.N., M.S.N., rheumatology nurse specialist, was very helpful with Marycely's chapter. Dr. Thomas Lehman's lecture on lupus at the Hospital for Special Surgery in New York gave me a better understanding of this complicated disease.

At Gillette Children's Hospital in St. Paul, Minnesota, I would like to thank Joseph M. Manion, M.A., former Director of Public Relations and Medical Media Services, as well as Tim McNeely, his associate. Barbara J. Clayman put me in touch with Britta Nicholson and her family, and was a generous host throughout my several trips to Minneapolis. Thanks also to Lawrence Kutner for his help. I hope you all read his wonderful syndicated *New York Times* column, "Parent and Child." Dr. Don Brunnquell is with the Minneapolis Children's Medical Center and, like Dr. Stephen Hersh mentioned earlier, works with children who have critical illnesses. He provided me with valuable insights and, more important, called my attention to a book that ended up being my most valuable medical reference tool: *Issues in the Care of Children with Chronic Illness* by Nicholas Hobbs and James B. Perrin. I highly recommend this book to anyone interested in the issues of chronic illness. It can be ordered directly from the publisher: Jossey-Bass Publishers, 350 Fansome Street, San Francisco, California 94104.

One interesting chapter in the Hobbs-Perrin book is "The Constant Shadow" by Robert Massie, Jr., who was the subject of a poignant book by his parents, Robert and Suzanne Massie. It tells the story of their son's struggle and extraordinary courage growing up with hemophilia. Bobby Massie, after graduating from Princeton University and Yale Divinity School, entered the ministry. He is now married and the father of a two-year-old son. We spent a day at New York Hospital while he was having his yearly checkup, which included a battery of tests. Many of the families in the waiting room, most of whom had young sons with hemophilia, recognized him because for them his story had been a guiding light. One young mother, her eyes brimming with tears, said to Bobby: "Sometimes I think it's easier for my child than it is for me because he's never known anything different. I love my son so much but I hate this disease with all my heart and sometimes I have trouble separating the two." Bobby put his arm around her and said that he knew how she felt but that her son was so much more fortunate than he had been, to be facing this illness now when so many advances had been made. "It's sort of like early boot camp," he said. "If you go through it and come out OK, you're really in pretty good shape to deal with practically anything that comes along later." It's a message that I won't forget and I doubt if that young woman will either.

Besides putting me in touch with both Dr. Perrin and Bobby Massie, it was Dr. Brunnquell who gave me the encouragement I needed to reaffirm my initial intuition that a book such as this, dealing with a wide variety of medical illnesses and disabilities, would be a valuable resource. He told me about a study done by Vanderbilt University, which basically said that 85 percent of all the emotional problems experienced by families dealing with chronic illness were *non-disease specific*. This was what I had felt from the onset and it was reassuring for me to find that a concept I had felt only instinctively had been articulated by such a respected medical institution. From the beginning I had hoped this book would deal more with the issues related to medical illness than with the individual illnesses themselves. It is my hope that each of the wise and illuminating voices of the fourteen children heard in these pages will be useful in some way.

In Boston, my gratitude goes to Dr. James Perrin at Massachusetts General Hospital; Dr. Peter Greenspan at General Medical Associates; and Nora Wells, a staff member at the Federation for Children with Special Needs, a valuable resource, I think, for families reading this book. The address is 312 Stuart Street, Boston, Massachusetts 02116 (617-482-2915).

As always, I would have been lost without the able assistance of Carol Atkinson, who transcribed all my tapes with speed and great care. I am grateful to Dr. William Chambers, Dr. Eda LeShan, Frank Deford, William Zinsser, Dr. Michael Lewis, Reena Feldman, Laura Perry, Brenda Steere, Patty Francy, and my husband, Kurt Vonnegut, for their encouragement and helpful suggestions. Betsy Pitha is one of the best copy editors it has been my good fortune with whom to work.

I could not have done this book without the diligent help of my editorial assistant, Peggy Guthart, who worked with me from beginning to end. It was our good fortune that her grandfather, Dr. Wilfred Carrol, was a constant source of information and advice.

It is here that I would like to acknowledge two young people who inspired me to undertake this project. One is Bruno Navasky, who in

1979 was diagnosed with a tumor in his chest, was hospitalized on and off for a year and a half, and spent many hours talking to me about his experience. He is now a very healthy twenty-two-year-old Harvard graduate on his way to Japan. The other person is Amanda Gershon, whom I met when she was only nine. A beautiful and intelligent child with cystic fibrosis, she was seated next to me at a luncheon honoring Rosalynn Carter. We kept in touch until her death last year, at the age of seventeen. There was never a moment while I was writing this book when I was not conscious of the sensitive insights Bruno and Amanda shared with me.

Finally, my deepest and heartfelt appreciation must go the fourteen wonderful, special families whose stories are set down on these pages. You have made me realize more than ever what matters. I am indebted to you for sharing your lives so others may benefit. I thank you for teaching me about love and courage and a compelling faith in the future. It has been a privilege for me to have written this book. It has been an honor for me to have known each one of you.

JK

JILL KREMENTZ works as a journalist, photographer, and portraitist and is the author-photographer of twenty award-winning books for children.

Her previous books in this series, *How It Feels When a Parent Dies, How It Feels to Be Adopted,* and *How It Feels When Parents Divorce,* have been praised by educators, doctors, and sociologists as invaluable contributions to their fields because of the author's ability to communicate with children and draw from them their truest thoughts and feelings.

Ms. Krementz is the 1984 recipient of the *Washington Post/* Children's Book Guild Nonfiction Award for "creatively produced works that make a difference." She lives in New York City with her husband, author Kurt Vonnegut, and their young daughter, Lily.